MAKING THE SCENE
IN THE GARDEN STATE

MAKING THE SCENE IN THE GARDEN STATE

Popular Music in New Jersey from Edison to Springsteen and Beyond

DEWAR MacLEOD

R

RUTGERS UNIVERSITY PRESS
New Brunswick, Camden, and Newark, New Jersey, and London

Library of Congress Cataloging-in-Publication Data

Names: MacLeod, Dewar, 1962—author.
Title: Making the scene in the Garden State: popular music in New Jersey
     from Edison to Springsteen and beyond / Dewar MacLeod.
Description: New Brunswick: Rutgers University Press, [2020] |
     Includes bibliographical references and index.
Identifiers: LCCN 2019020423 | ISBN 9780813574660 (cloth)
Subjects: LCSH: Popular music—New Jersey—History and criticism. |
     Sound recording industry—New Jersey—History.
Classification: LCC ML3477.7.N55 M3 2020 | DDC 781.6409749—dc23
LC record available at https://lccn.loc.gov/2019020423

A British Cataloging-in-Publication record for this book is available
from the British Library.

www.rutgersuniversitypress.org

Manufactured in the United States of America

For Sinéad and Rory

CONTENTS

MAKING THE SCENE
IN THE GARDEN STATE

INTRODUCTION

Making Scenes

Beyond its reputations as the suburban outpost to Manhattan, the industrial wasteland, the barren swamps and pinelands where gangsters dump their victims, propagator of the tacky and déclassé, pathway between far more interesting locales, New Jersey has been home to vital and exciting scenes of musical production and enjoyment.

New Jersey deserves its own musical history. The state has been home not simply to musicians who were born there, but also to those who went off to seek fame in the bright lights of the big city. The state has fostered and grown local scenes of musical and historical import. Certainly, its location on the outskirts of major cities at the northern and southern ends has factored into New Jersey's influence. But this book will explore the homegrown and nurtured musical production and consumption in New Jersey. The book will fill in the historical record by including some vibrant and important musical moments that have not received due attention. But I am interested in even more than claiming historical space for these musical productions as worthy of inclusion in some sort of musical hall of fame—my interest lies in the social history of the ways in which people produce and consume music. Accordingly, the organizing conceit of this book is the concept of scenes.

I use the term "scene" to discuss a variety of types of historical groupings of people around music, "the contexts in which clusters of producers, musicians, and fans collectively share their common musical tastes and collectively distinguish themselves from others."[1] Over the past few decades, scholars have explored "the production, performance, and reception of popular music. Work in the scenes perspective focuses on situations where performers, support facilities, and fans come together to collectively create music for their own enjoyment."[2] The term itself is malleable, even slippery, used as it is by participants, journalists, and scholars, often in very different ways.

My research for this book has come from distinctly different kinds of sources, depending on the type of scene I was researching. Sometimes the major factors involve the technology and business aspects of making music. Other scenes are fraught with contestation over meaning and deeply invested in signification, identity, and community. Scenes are places where people come together to create a new experience of music that cannot be found elsewhere, and the ultimate product is a piece of music that reaches beyond the space.

The list of terms for thinking about scenes is extensive: music worlds, subcultures, networks, communities, fan communities, taste communities, youth culture, tribes, and neotribes. And the ways of thinking about scenes are even more vast and varied. They involve the examination of creativity, aesthetics, infrastructure, communications, commerce, geography, identity, fields and discourses, mass culture, and so on.

"Music," John Blacking writes, "is essentially about aesthetic experiences and the creative expression of individual human beings in community, about the sharing of feelings and ideas."[3] The interaction between aesthetics, creative expression, identity, community, feelings, and ideas forms the basis for my explorations of scenes.

Scholarship on scenes descends most directly from work on subcultures and youth culture in the 1970s, especially from the so-called Birmingham School at the Centre for Contemporary Cultural Studies (CCCS), which explored how people came together to create identities and communities in opposition to and in dialogue with the mass culture of capitalist society, combining ethnography, sociology, structuralist and post-structuralist literary theory to create the new field of cultural studies.[4] The work coming out of the Birmingham School was extremely influential and inspired a generation of scholars in cultural studies, especially in the United States and England, to undertake theoretically infused, deep, microsociological, ethnographic examinations of local communities within the contexts of class, race, gender, and other structural determinants of identity.

By the 1990s, "post-subcultures" scholars had begun to criticize subculture as too static and fixed, arguing that individual identities are more constructed and fluid, and cultural groups are better seen as fluid entities built around life-styles, rather than fixed groups that represent social class.[5] The Birmingham School was derided for a romanticized vision of "working-class youth subcultures 'heroically' resisting subordination through 'semiotic guerrilla warfare'" in favor of a "more pragmatic approach" reflecting a belief that "the potential for style itself to resist appears largely lost."[6] Scholars turned away from subcultures to "channels" or "subchannels," "temporary substream networks," "neo-tribes," and "clubcultures"—less ambitious terms that reflect a "post-heroic" vision that makes more limited claims about identity and community rather than social transformation or revolution.[7] Scenes can be united across space through shared tastes and social and economic networks, allowing members to define themselves through identification and differentiation.

Recently scholars have embraced and expanded the concept of scene to capture myriad types of cultural activity and social experiences, in seeking to find "a way of talking about the roles of place, participation and circula-tion in the production of popular music . . . [and] the field of social relations in which music circulated."[8] A "scenes perspective" emerged within cultural studies to explore the ways in which "doing scene" is "both extraordinarily creative and an ordinary, practical accomplishment."[9] Building on the pio-neering theorizing of Will Straw, Barry Shank, and others in the 1990s, later scholars have called for "scene thinking," arguing that "naming a group or cluster of activity a scene says something about how these concrete practices and spaces disclose the social's inherent relationality."[10]

Looking at scenes allows us to explore both the creative and the quotid-ian, the ways in which meaning and identity are formed, and the social worlds, both local and global, in which they take place.[11] Scenes "provide systems of identification and connection, while simultaneously inviting acts of novelty, invention and innovation. Scenes are set within the fabric of everyday life but also function as an imagined alternative to the ordinary, work-a-day world."[12] Although the concept of scene might be "ambiguous" or even "downright confusing," scene thinking defines not a thing, but a perspective, a way of looking at the relationships between individuals and institutions in a given setting.[13] The concept of scene, because of its attention to space, is more flex-ible than subculture or fandom.[14] A scene has a degree of self-consciousness about collective identity; it pulls people and ideas together in spaces that create coherence; people in the scene actively participate in types of work and productivity; a scene is a place for working out rules, identities, tastes, and politics both internally and vis-à-vis the outside world; a scene registers transformation and historical memory, change and continuity; the scene mediates between the personal and the social, the private and the public, turning creativity into cultural activity, and cultural activity into social engagement.[15] The concept of scenes is necessarily flexible and expansive because the range of activities that takes place is so wide, and all those actors and acts must be examined by their very connections.

WHY MUSIC?

Scenes can gather around any group of people or activity, but so often music provides the centerpiece. So, the question needs to be asked: Why music?

Music matters because "musical participation and experience are valuable for the processes of personal and social integration that make us whole."[16] Anthropologists and philosophers have explored how "the arts are essential to human survival because they serve the function of integrating different parts of the self and integrating individuals with each other and their environment."[17] Experiencing music, in particular, brings to the foreground "the crucial interplay between the Possible and the Actual."[18] It is through music that we experience both personal ideals and relationships as well as flow or even the total erasure of self and merging with others. Music is deeply emotional and personal, and at the same time social, collective, spontaneous, and public. We sing lullabies to babies, dance in discotheques, and bask in symphonic sounds in the concert hall.[19]

Simon Frith, perhaps our greatest pop music sociologist, argues for evaluating popular music and culture aesthetically, not just socially. "The question we should be asking," he writes, "is not what does popular music *reveal* about 'the people' but how does it *construct* them."[20] But pop music does its work in social situations. People create their sense of identity through their musical choices, choosing social groups and gathering together in audiences of collective identity. And they navigate the divide between private and public through song. Love songs, for example, Frith writes, "give shape and voice to emotions that otherwise cannot be expressed without embarrassment or incoherence. . . . These songs do not replace our conversations—pop singers do not do our courting for us—but they make our feelings seem richer and more convincing than we can make them appear in our own words, even to ourselves."[21] We attach ourselves to singers because they say what we would say if we had the ability: "It is as if we get to know ourselves via the music."[22] From there, we, as fans, come to "possess" the music; "we make it part of our own identity and build it into our sense of ourselves."[23] Through this process, we move from personal taste to social identity through our connection to music.

Producing and enjoying music, therefore, are always social acts, even when we are alone. We are "acting in concert" and participating in community.[24] A musical community provides "a sense of belonging and shared affiliation around notions of class, ethnicity, style, and taste expressed through music and other creative cultural expressions."[25] Musical communities develop from local face-to-face interactions over time, and they develop ideological, affective, and imagined dimensions, including cultural memory and a shared sense of solidarity. But, like all communities, they can be fragmentary, ad hoc, and fleeting.[26] These musical communities are situated within global and transnational networks "at the intersection of local and mass consumption."[27] Communities can even share culture across time and space, and what appear to be "highly separate, distinctive, and clearly bonded local scenes" can make up "a singular and relatively coherent movement whose translocal connections [are] of greater significance than its local differences."[28] The connections through identities, tastes, travel, technology, commerce, and media serve to create "a complex translocal network of 'concrete' connections which [function] to construct and support the strength of subjective identity and the consistent and distinctive tastes."[29]

Starting in the 1950s, in his nuanced ethnographic work on jazz and dance communities, Howard Becker introduced the dimensions of place and space into the examination of musical worlds. Becker defined a place not only as physical space but also by its social definitions, the shared expectations and activities, and the larger social and economic contexts that define the opportunities and limits to activity. Becker provided deep and rich work on the gigging economy, the everydayness of the ways jazz musicians worked and played, and one of the key elements was place: "Most of the time we played what the 'place'—the combination of physical space and social and financial arrangements—made possible."[30] As a musician himself, he was highly attuned to the fact that often the most important factor in defining the art of jazz was not esoteric, but economic (which was itself political, social, highly personal, and local).

Subcultural or scene spaces are important as places for "unconventional social groups" to enact their "way of life" beyond simply recreation.[31] For some scenes, those spaces exist beyond the club, in recording studios, and also in apartments, bars, squats, and DIY (do it yourself) venues. Jazz, for example, cannot be understood without attention to spatial practices, both in terms of the particularities of space and political economy in locales (the cities of New Orleans, New York, Memphis, Chicago, etc.) and institutions (clubs, studios, after-hours venues, etc.).[32] The scene is also historical, as spaces and places change, whereas participants create and harbor memories and newcomers continually renew and transform the scene. Music is often created out of the mainstream, in the counter-public sphere as well as "disrespectable" and "impure spaces."[33] These liminal spaces are not easily classified or policed because they exist on the margins, in the interstices.[34] In these marginal and "in-between" spaces, the hierarchical social boundaries are challenged, and individuals and groups create new musics, but also new selves, new collaborations, and ways of thinking about and ordering society.[35] The momentary disruptions provided by this "carnivalistic environment" threaten to break down barriers and hierarchies, with all the attendant anxieties and opportunities that brings.[36]

Some scholars have adopted the term *musicking* to describe the varied practices that make up the social elements of a music scene, such as composing, creating, rehearsing, performing, listening, dancing, and so forth. The scene includes the ticket-takers, bouncers, bartenders, sound technicians, and roadies, as well as the musicians and fans.[37] The process of *musicking* allows for the genius of inspiration and creativity, but also accounts for an array of individuals, both professional and amateur, partaking in writing, composing, playing, dancing, singing, listening, producing, and so on—many of them invisible to outsiders as "the unseen scene."[38] Situated within the symbiotic and synergistic aspects of social relationships, the music then takes on meaning in the moments of exchange between musician and listener, moments that can be extremely intense and intimate, even transcendent and spiritual.[39]

Improvisation, for example, emerges from the scene, linking the local (liberatory and exploratory) within global musical and social contexts.[40] Set within the community of musicians, improvisation resists the co-optation of mass culture and gives form to the basic impulses at the heart of scenes, connecting individual expression and virtuosity to community, with deep historical roots, as a kind of "empathic communication across time."[41] The music gives voice to alternatives, possibilities, and utopian impulses that emerge in daily life and social relations within the scene.

We need to see scene participants as historical actors, often articulate and quite aware of their own concepts, innovations, tropes, and lexicons. And we should see them both within their music spaces and the larger social and spatial environments.[42]

Musical scenes are built on the intellectual and creative labor of writers, artists, performers, producers, engineers, inventors, and entrepreneurs, as well as fans, and that creativity is what brings everyone out and together.[43] All art is produced within social contexts, so even to examine an individual text is to explicate the world from which it came. As Becker writes, "Art worlds rather than artists make art."[44]

Being a part of a scene is sometimes a matter of work, its conditions and processes, which are routine as well as exciting.[45] Musicians work within a variety of settings, their careers dependent on many variables, individuals, and institutions.

People and institutions other than musicians also contribute to the formation of the scene. Influenced by the theoretical work of Michel DeCerteau, scholars studied fandom as "automatically more than the mere act of being a fan of something; it was a collective strategy, a communal effort to form interpretive communities that in their subcultural cohesion evaded the preferred and intended meanings of the 'power bloc' presented by popular media."[46] As with the study of subcultures, an initial wave of study of fandom as oppositional was supplemented by scholarship that explored the internal dynamics and hierarchies of fan communities and their links to larger social and cultural relations. Following Bourdieu's notion of "cultural capital" in the sociology of consumption, this perspective is less likely to see fan communities as sites of autonomy, emancipation, resistance, and subversion than as arenas for working out relations with peers, the larger world, and everyday life.[47] As recent scholars of fandom explain, "Studying fan audiences allows us to explore some of the key mechanisms through which we interact with the mediated world at the heart of our social, political, and cultural realities and identities. Perhaps the most important contribution of contemporary research into fan audiences thus lies in furthering our understanding of how we form emotional bonds with ourselves and others in a modern, mediated world."[48]

Scholars are extending the concept to explore a range of social phenomena that do not fit the traditional subculture definition, so that "rather than drawing a hard line between scenes and nonscenes it may be more appropriate to say that groups exhibit varying degrees of 'sceneness.'"[49] Fans of Kate Bush, for example, were relatively "invisible" and "unspectacular," even discrete in their fandom, but they still exhibited "a strong degree of shared feelings . . . and a quest for distinction" that united them despite multiple obstacles.[50]

The work on fans takes us back to the individual relationship to music. In *Performing Rites: On the Value of Popular Music*—the very title signaling his perspective—Simon Frith explores the folk worlds and folk rituals of popular music communities, the ways that music connects to resistance, escape, reconciliation, and transformation.[51] For Frith, the act of "'listening' itself is a performance: to understand how musical pleasure, meaning, and evaluation work, we have to understand how, as listeners, we perform the music for ourselves."[52] Performance is social and communicative; it requires an audience that is always interpretive, conveying and making meaning.[53] "Music's enveloping effect" captures both the performer and the audience.[54]

That special feeling that comes from music makes it seem that the specialness derives from the music itself; but the experience of music—even the solitary experience of music—is social.[55] We just do not necessarily feel it as such. We feel it as personal and sensual, in our bodies, in the flow, as "pleasure in motion."[56] We form bonds with others, merge with them, even on the dance floor, in the concert hall, even alone in our bedrooms, through our emotional identification with music in specific settings and situations.[57] When we listen to music, we engage in the immediate experience, but also in the reflective, abstract act of judging, so that we find our way in the world, both in the moment and in the larger scheme of things.[58] Through the performance of music, at least for the time being, things make sense, ethically, sensually, emotionally, and socially.[59] Music both takes us out of ourselves and our boring lives into imagined worlds and makes us who we are "through the experiences it offers of the body, time, and sociability, experiences which enable us to place ourselves in imaginative cultural narratives."[60] Music integrates our aesthetics and ethics. "Identity is necessarily a matter of ritual: it describes one's place in a dramatized pattern of relationships—one can never really express oneself 'autonomously,'" Frith writes. "Self-identity is cultural identity."[61]

Music shapes our identity, music makes us feel human, music brings us together. But music can also alienate and divide us; it can also "feed disaffection and create spaces of alterity."[62] Think of the longing the perfect love song evokes. Think of the tribal conflicts between different scenes. But even within a scene, the identification with music is ultimately based on a shared sense of difference.

Barry Shank, one of the pioneering theorists and historians of scenes, has explored musical beauty as a psychological and political phenomenon, charting how the deeply personal experience of engaging with music connects to social and political understandings in complex ways. He focuses on how "the act of musical listening enables us to confront complex and mobile structures of impermanent relationships—the sonic interweaving of tones and beats, upper harmonics, and contrasting timbres—that model the experience of belonging to a community not of unity, but of difference."[63] How does that feeling of difference relate to engagement in the social and the political?

Others have written about the relationships between music and politics and social movements, but often music is just a vehicle to explore political consciousness and community. Shank wants to discover

> how music . . . enacts its own force, creating shared senses of the world. The experience of musical beauty confirms within its listeners the sense that this moment of listening has within it the promise of things being right, of pieces fitting together, of wholes emerging out of so much more than the assembled riffs and rhythms. That affect is powerful. . . . When we hear the exquisite combination of right sonic relations, of auditory sensations of tension and release, of concentrated effects of sounding pressure and muscular response, we sense a commonality that feels right, that announces that this *we* that we are at this moment is the right *we*, the *we* that we are meant to be.[64]

Shank describes that perfect feeling of being at one with the music and with fellow music lovers. But then he takes it away: "Of course, that is not literally true." We do not, after all, really agree with our colleagues on all the important things; in fact, we might disagree severely about both what the music means and what the larger project we think we are involved in means. For Shank, "the coexistence of a feeling of unity and shared beauty with the knowledge that those with whom we are sharing that feeling can and do disagree with us on deeply fundamentally important matters" forms the basis for understanding that a musical community is based not on sameness, but on difference.[65] His focus on beauty reminds us it is the aesthetic that reveals and constructs political power. A shared sense of the beautiful forms the basis for a political grouping, as "the experience of beauty is the recognition of the way things could be, the way things should be. The ability to produce beauty, therefore, is an index of the ability to imagine a better future."[66]

"Music provides us," Shank writes, "with primary evidence that we are not solitary beings, that our innermost selves are interwoven with others."[67] But we listen socially, with genres as conventions that capture the historical and social aspects of listening and interpreting, so that even on the dance floor together, we feel a sense of connection and community that is different for each of us.[68] We are, therefore, always engaged in "a constant tracking back and forth between sounds and imagined others. We can never not do that."[69] Through our participation with music, we join the sonic and the social.

THE CHAPTERS

Chapter 1, "Thomas Edison and the First Recording Studio," explores the first place that people came together to record music, Thomas Edison's laboratory in West Orange, New Jersey. Edison's phonograph, invented in 1877, dramatically altered the ways that musicians and listeners could engage with music. For the first time, sound was captured for all to hear for all time. The chapter explores the process of developing the technology and space for recording. Many scholars have examined the history of recording technology and some have documented the discography of the Edison cylinders, but few have looked at the experience and the social history of how the first place for music recording developed. Edison's studio created a music world for a new way of engaging with making and listening to music.

Chapter 2, "The Victor Talking Machine Company and the Scene at Home," details Emile Berliner's invention of the flat disc gramophone, which became the basis for the Victor Talking Machine Company founded in 1901. With its globally recognized logo, Nipper, the marketing of the Victrola, and the creation of celebrity recording artists, Victor attracted musical artists as diverse as Enrico Caruso, Paul Robeson, the Carter Family, and Jimmie Rodgers, who flocked to Camden, New Jersey, to put their sounds on cylinders in the first decades of the twentieth century. At Victor's studios in Camden, singers and musicians created a new type of recording artist. And the Victrola signaled a new type of domestic scene, as middle-class consumers increasingly shaped their identities through their engagement with the commercially available products in the privacy of their own homes.

Chapter 3, "Jazz at the Cliffside: The Studios of Rudy Van Gelder," tells the story of the recording sessions in the legendary studios in Hackensack and Englewood Cliffs, New Jersey, where some of the most innovative and influential jazz of the twentieth century was recorded. Rudy Van Gelder's distinctive recording style lured artists such as John Coltrane, Miles Davis, and Thelonious Monk to his studios for musical exploration and innovation for Blue Note, Prestige, and other important postwar jazz record labels. The music world that developed in Van Gelder's studios was distinctive both for its sound and its ambience.

Chapter 4, "Transylvanian Bandstand and Rockin' with the Cool Ghoul," explores the television dance show *Disc-O-Teen*, hosted by Zacherley, the Cool Ghoul, and broadcast on UHF Channel 47. The show brought young people from Newark and the surrounding suburbs together to dance to the latest hits and to local garage bands in the 1960s. Teens gathered every afternoon to dance on television, and other kids raced home after school to watch the proceedings with Zacherley and their favorite dancers. The teen scene at *Disc-O-Teen* took place within a larger context of the post-Beatlemania garage band explosion. Kids picked up guitars and played rock music in high schools throughout New Jersey (and across America). Young people's identities were formed within the context of the local and national communities of rock culture in the 1960s.

Chapter 5, "The Upstage Club and the Asbury Park Scene," describes the thriving rock scene at the Upstage Club before Bruce Springsteen ("The Boss") made the Asbury Park club The Stone Pony famous. From 1968 to 1971, the club hosted jam sessions by young local rockers like The Boss and Southside Johnny and a generation of up-and-coming musicians. In the late 1960s, the era of Woodstock, increasing intergenerational tensions over the Vietnam War along with riots in ghettos across the nation caused young people to embrace rock culture as a unifying element in opposition to mainstream culture. At the Upstage Club, the focus was music as escape from society and into artistic and individual expression.

Chapter 6, "'Drums Along the Hudson': The Hoboken Sound" details the history of the scene in Hoboken in the 1980s and 1990s. The club Maxwell's in Hoboken played host to thousands of local and touring punk, alternative, and indie bands from its opening in 1978 to its closing in 2013, forging an important stop on the "cultural underground railroad" of the indie music scene. Young people were no longer united generationally, but a subculture developed that unified some segments of youth through a shared taste in music and a shared DIY sensibility. The scene at Hoboken was central to the shaping of identity for local musicians and fans, as well as touring artists from the United States and the United Kingdom.

The conclusion explores the multiple music scenes in my hometown in northern New Jersey to demonstrate how music worlds continue to develop and thrive.

1 · THOMAS EDISON AND THE FIRST RECORDING STUDIO

Humans have always gathered to make and enjoy music, but it was in a laboratory in New Jersey that they first came together to record music. When Thomas Edison spoke the words "Mary had a little lamb" into a tube in 1877, he started the process that would transform the way in which people assembled to make and enjoy music. One of the signal achievements in the creation of modernity started with an act of music. "I was singing to the mouth-piece of a telephone," Thomas Edison remembered, "when the vibrations of the voice sent the fine steel point into my finger. That set me to thinking. If I could record the actions of the point and send the point over the same surface afterward, I saw no reason why the thing would not talk." Thus, by "merest accident," as he set to work on improving the telephone, Edison ushered the modern age of musical recording.[1] At the same time, Edison never fully grasped the cultural implications of his invention. Always the scientist and technician, he resisted seeing the ways that his innovations transformed the ways people engaged with music and the entertainment marketplace. Although the first scene of recorded music makers developed in New Jersey, it did so under the guidance of a man steadfastly old-fashioned in his tastes and approach to culture.

Already a prolific and famous inventor—dubbed the Wizard of Menlo Park that very year—Edison was working on an improvement to the telephone when it struck him that the sound waves he was generating could be made to vibrate a diaphragm that would move a sharp object to engrave the waves onto a surface. He was not the first with this insight—Edouard-Leon Scott de Martinville had devised a "phonautograph" in 1857, which transcribed sound waves onto paper, and Charles Cros filed a patent remarkably similar to Edison's at nearly the same time.[2] But Edison's original insight was not in the speaking or the recording but in the playing back. He wrote in his notebook on July 18, 1877, "There is no doubt that I shall be able to store up and reproduce accurately at any future time the human voice perfectly."[3] Edison's phonograph was "wonderfully simple," without the need for electrical transformation that the phone required.[4] "I was never so taken aback in my life. Everybody was astonished. I was always afraid of things that worked the first time," Edison recalled.[5] It is fitting that he spoke a nursery rhyme, completing the couplet, "Mary had a little lamb / Its fleece was white as snow." The words were not quite prose, but not quite music either, fitting because the musical future of the machine was not clear right away.

Edison himself foresaw, as was his nature, the business uses of the phonograph (a name, by the way, that came from a long list Edison drew up, its choice nearly random). When Edison presented his machine to the public, he listed a number of uses for it, among which music came in at number 4. Certainly, recording technology would develop over the years for a variety of uses, but ultimately music made the phonograph's place in history.

Imagine the strangeness of it all. For all of human history, sound had come out live, right in front of you, in sync with the objects in your vision. Or sound came from a distance, signaling danger approaching or nature at work. Music was enjoyed face-to-face, as humans gathered around the campfire or the piano in the parlor, or on the stage they were viewing. For decades at least, people had begun imagining other possibilities. The music theorist Moritz Hauptmann called for "musical photographs."[6] Édouard-Léon Scott de Martinville had transcribed the musical waves onto paper, "recording" sounds that would not become available until the invention of twenty-first-century technologies. Now, in this age of miraculous technological inventions, the most miraculous inventor himself could make music, singing into the tube and recording his voice on a piece of tinfoil that could then be made to repeat his singing, warts and all, for all to hear.

Music was not the first purpose of the phonograph. Everywhere he went, Edison exhibited its power as a "talking" or "speaking" machine, a wondrous invention of the industrial age that would capture sound, but would also take on a life of its own in talking back at listeners. How could the world not be a different place when such a fundamental rule of physics had now been over-thrown? Before the phonograph, according to one historian, "every sonic phenomenon had possessed a unity of time and space; it occurred once, for a certain duration, in one place, and then it was gone forever. By embedding time in objects and making possible what the economist Jacques Attali has called the stockpiling of sound, recording technology destroyed that uniqueness."[7]

"What would have become of such a man in the days of the Salem witch-craft?" asked a reporter upon viewing Edison's demonstration of the phono-graph in 1878.[8] Indeed, how magical, maybe more magical than all the others, was this invention, to take an ephemeral sound and capture it? Writers searched for words to describe the process—sounds were "etched" or "impris-oned" or "preserved or bottled up, as it were, and kept for future use"[9]—but none fully conveyed the impossibility of it all. "The *New York Sun* was fasci-nated by the metaphysical implications of an invention that could play 'Echoes from Dead Voices,'" according to the historian Randall Stross. And, "The *New York Times* predicted that a large business would develop in 'bot-tled sermons,' and wealthy connoisseurs would take pride in keeping a 'well-stocked oratorical cellar.'"[10] One writer claimed that the Marine Band was "rendering itself immortal . . . by having its most harmonious strains bottled in large quantities."[11] The Reverend Horatio Nelson Powers claimed to "hoard music and speech."[12] Edison himself boldly declared that he had achieved "the captivity of all manner of sound-waves heretofore designated as 'fugi-tive' and their permanent retention."[13] In what may have seemed more threat than promise, he told the public:

> Your words, for example, are preserved in tin foil, and will come back upon the application of the instrument years after you are dead in exactly the same tone of voice you spoke them in. . . . This tongue-less, toothless instrument, with-out larynx or pharynx, dumb voiceless matter, nevertheless mimics your tones, speaks with your voice, utters your words, and centuries after you have crum-bled into dust will repeat again and again, to a generation that could never know you, every idle thought, every fond fancy, every vain word that you choose to whisper against this thin iron diaphragm.[14]

Upon hearing this pronouncement from Edison, the reporter "thought of that passage of Holy Writ which says, 'every idle thought and every vain word which man thinks or utters are recorded in the Judgment Book.' Does the Recording Angel sit beside a Celestial Phonograph, against whose spiritual diaphragm some mysterious ether presses the record of a human life?"[15] This was no mere technical achievement. This still-imperfect, this (in Edison's own words) "poor specimen of a phonograph," threatened to change not only human history, but the hereafter as well.[16]

No wonder the public wrestled with just what manner of man this Edison was, and just what he wrought. "It sounds more like the devil every time," claimed one listener at Edison's 1888 demonstration to the National Academy of Sciences.[17] One writer made the connection to Emerson's thoughts on the invention of the daguerreotype: "We make the sun paint our portraits now, and by-and-by we shall *organize the echoes* as we now organize the shadows."[18] Edison wondered if the bigoted and ignorant might not "destroy the machine as an invention of the devil and mob the agents as his regular imps."[19]

Taking full advantage of his proximity to New York and his skyrocketing fame, Edison made the rounds of scientific circles and the publicity accorded by the city's newspaper and magazine industries. Riding the train from Menlo Park to the city, tinfoil-covered machine in tow, he visited the offices of *Scientific American* to have his machine vetted, and word of its wonders broadcast to the scientific community and beyond. People came from all over the world to meet the Wizard. Edison welcomed interesting visitors and loved engaging in conversation, often sparring and joking with journalists (whom he loved to fool with his "Wizard" persona).[20] Reporters made the trek to the New Jersey hinterlands on special trains arranged by the Pennsylvania Railroad to find the inventor and his crew in the laboratory, tinkering with improvements, Edison harmonizing on "John Brown's Body" with one of his workmen.[21]

Nearly all stories of Edison from that time begin with the journey out to visit the Wizard. Very quickly, the now-legendary biography of the boy inventor and entrepreneur became a standard part of the story, followed by an investigation into Edison the Man, the Scientist, the Wizard. He loved to put on the "Great Inventor" act for reporters, but all who met and worked with him were genuinely intrigued and charmed by "the happy-hooligan light out of his gray eyes."[22] One visitor recalled, "On meeting him one is first astonished by the extreme buoyancy of his step and his bearing. . . . His large head and twinkling eyes give the immediate impression of intense vitality."[23] When the writer George Parsons Lathrop visits Edison in 1890, he finds a man who "is always absolutely himself. He does not present to one's observation a mixture of superficial manners and concealed inner man. . . . He has, in a degree which is literally startling, the power of self-concentration."[24] Edison told Lathrop that he invented the phonograph by "logical deduction," but Lathrop also noticed "mingled abstraction and fire" in Edison's face and the "imaginative aspect of his mind."[25]

Fearing that he would be accused of ventriloquism, or worse, Edison took pains to separate himself from the wizards and magicians and hucksters who trod the stage, especially since charlatans and con men were legion in nineteenth-century popular culture.[26] When Kentucky senator James B. Beck spoke into the machine during Edison's visit to the Senate chamber, he heard back his own words, "I don't believe in you, I think you are a humbug."[27] One of his chemists later recalled, "Edison himself was generally referred to as The Old Man. He had nicknamed his experimenters 'Muckers,' he himself being the chief Mucker. . . . Edison shrank from the word genius because of its suggestion of a miraculous power of creating by mere inspiration something out of nothing."[28]

But at the same time, Edison loved the dramatic demonstration, mixing the cornpone with his "wizard-like air."[29] Another visitor captured the awe of arriving in the middle of the night to find Edison in his element, "a midnight workman with supernal forces whose mysterious phenomena have taught me their largest idea of elemental power; a modern alchemist, who finds the philosopher's stone to be made of carbon, and with his magnetic wand changes every-day knowledge into the pure gold of new applications and original uses. He is THOMAS A. EDISON, at work in his laboratory, deep in his conjuring of Nature while the world sleeps."[30]

The public could not help but embrace with awe the invention's "moral side, a stirring, optimistic inspiration," but Edison emphasized the practical and scientific nature of the phonograph, promising its use for business and literature.[31] He forecast the day when all the musics of the world would be captured and distributed widely, proclaiming, "We will phonograph orchestral concerts by brass and string bands, instrumental and vocal solos and part songs. The sheets bearing the sound impressions of this music will be removed from the phonograph and multiplied to any extent by electrotyping, and persons can make selections of any compositions they desire. Then this music may be reproduced by any phonograph, with all the original sweetness and expression; and not only that, but the pitch can be raised or lowered by increasing or diminishing the speed of the phonograph."[32]

Edison continued the rounds, visiting Washington, DC, in April 1878, stopping in at the National Academy of Sciences and the House Committee on Patents, meeting with President Rutherford Hayes in the White House in the middle of the night,[33] and sitting for Matthew Brady for photographic portraits—itself a fairly new and marvelous method of capturing the impermanent.[34] But soon, advances and opportunities in electric lighting grabbed Edison's attention and he dismissed the talking machine as "a mere toy, which has no commercial value."[35] As Roland Gelatt has noted, "The phonograph, in truth, had been launched prematurely."[36] The sounds emanating from the machine, as miraculous as the whole thing was, were not really faithful duplications—"in fact, to some extent it is a burlesque or parody of the human voice," wrote one wag at the time.[37]

Not until a decade later, prompted by competition and new developments in the production and use of the phonograph, did he return his attention to the phonograph in his new laboratory in West Orange, New Jersey. Other inventors were making incremental improvements in the machine—stylus, diaphragm, wax replacing tinfoil, motor—and a new marketplace for recorded music emerged. In 1888, he released the "Improved Phonograph" and then the "Perfected Phonograph"—a typically Edisonian bluff designed to reclaim a place in what was now a crowded field of inventors and entrepreneurs.[38] Edison threw the efforts of his company back into the phonograph, launching decades of innovation, competition, intrigue, industrial espionage, legal battles over patents and copyright, and financial skullduggery in the burgeoning recorded music business.[39] Investor money was poured into the creation of a new factory in West Orange, in part to build phonographs and cylinders for the new coin-slot music business, which began in 1889 when an entrepreneur hooked the phonograph up to four listening tubes, each with its own nickel slot.[40] Within a year taverns, saloons, and hotels across the country had installed machines for playing the latest in popular music, comic songs, monologues, whistling tunes, and hymns.[41] Music recording and distribution companies sprang up all over to provide the material for the booming industry.

West Orange as a site of musical creation began in 1887 when the eleven-year old-classical piano prodigy and sensation Josef Hofmann, who would be called the greatest pianist of his generation, stopped in on his U.S. tour to record some cylinders.[42] Soon after, the famous German musician Hans von Bülow visited Edison. As reported in London in the *Musical Times and Sing-*

Thomas A. Edison and others with the "perfected" wax-recording phonograph, circa 1892. Edison is seated in the center, with Fred Ott at the left and Col. George Gouraud at the right. Standing (left to right) are W. K. L. Dickson, Charles Batchelor, A. Theodore Wangemann, John Ott, and Charles Brown. (Library of Congress Prints and Photographs Division.)

ing Class Circular, after recording a pianoforte, Bülow placed the tubes in his ears, "now a look of surprise creeps over his features, his face becomes ashy pale, he staggers back from the machine exclaiming, 'Mein Gott! Mein Gott! It is bewitched.' Recovering from what was almost a faint, he begs to be sent home at once, saying that his nerves are completely unstrung, and he must have rest."[43]

Ambivalent about the entertainment uses of the phonograph, Edison preferred to focus on the phonograph as a dictation machine for business. In the January 1891 inaugural issue of the National Phonograph Association's trade publication the *Phonogram*, Edison emphasized the use of the phonograph in dictation for business and correspondence. He recognized that "through the facility with which it stores up and reproduces music of all sorts, or whistling and recitations, it can be employed to furnish constant

amusement to invalids, or to social assemblies, at receptions, dinners, etc.,"
but he makes no mention of the commercial possibilities of recorded
music.[44] Despite his reluctance, Edison threw his team's efforts into the
phonograph business, and thus into the cylinder production business. By
necessity, Edison became a musical majordomo over the next forty years.
Typically, he did it his way—with a faith in his own tastes and opinions
that surpassed stubbornness.

Edison, always keenly aware of the commercial implications of his inventions, was one of the earliest to recognize that recording and distributing the
cylinders for playing in the coin-in-the-slot machines provided an opportunity for considerable profit if mass production techniques could be worked
out.[45] But he steadfastly adhered to the belief that the phonograph was a talking *machine*, not an entertainment device, and even classified his phonograph with the scientific instruments at world's fairs, not the musical ones.[46]
The overarching theme is that Edison always saw the phonograph in scientific terms. Although a main part of his genius was always his ability to situate his technical innovations in the larger scheme of social and commercial
relations, with the phonograph a part of him remained stubbornly in the laboratory. Even the whole notion of a "perfected" phonograph makes it a scientific problem to be solved not a cultural or artistic one. Ultimately, this
would be the downfall of the business. It is not simply that he was wrong, so
much as he was oblivious or resistant to the forces beyond the technical that
were shaping the life of the machine.

Despite his narrow focus, his competitive spirit brought him back into the
business, and West Orange, New Jersey, thus became one of the first and most
important places in the world where people gathered to record music when
the Columbia Street Studio opened for experimental recording. Over the
course of the coming years, the Edison company would also have studios in
New York City to make it easier for working singers and musicians to record
during the day before their live shows at night. But Columbia Street remained
the main studio for experimentation and testing, producing daily recordings
for both the lab and the marketplace. "Early recording studios were anything
but glamorous dens of technological marvel and musical creativity," according to the historian Susan Schmidt Horning. "The first studios were actual
laboratories where inventors and mechanics experimented with various
methods of capturing sound."[47] Cylinders had to be recorded in bunches
because there was no method of mass reproduction. The recording studio

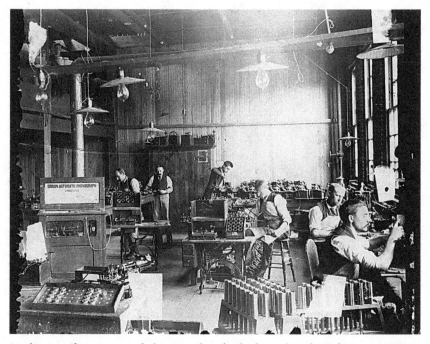

Production of coin-operated phonograph and cylinder in the Edison factory in West Orange, New Jersey, 1890. (Courtesy of Thomas Edison National Historical Park.)

was a laboratory, where Edison's staff "undertook extensive experimentation with a wide variety of instruments, recording horns, wax cylinder compounds, and methods of adjusting room acoustics."[48] Edison was famous, perhaps most of all, for his dogged experimental method, his willingness to try every method that popped into his mind, and in recording music, he stayed true to his process.[49]

It was in the recording studio, as Horning has noted, "that music began the shift from live performance art to a technologically mediated art."[50] And it was here that the first scene of performers who gathered to record was made, the first historical moment in which we can look at how the place of recording shaped the process of making music for the participants.

The experience of recording music during this acoustic era took some getting used to, and many artists resisted. There were no microphones or amplifiers. All sounds had to be poured into a cone-shaped horn, or series of horns, which funneled the sound waves down through a narrow opening to a diaphragm that vibrated a stylus needle that then etched a groove into

Music room, Building 5 of the Edison factory complex in West Orange, New Jersey, 1905. Left to right, Albert Kipfer, A. T. E. Wangemann, and George Boehme. (Courtesy of Thomas Edison National Historical Park.)

the wax on the cylinder. The horn worked like a backward megaphone, so that the singer placed his or her face into the wide mouth of the horn.[51] As one singer described the process, it was like "singing with a muzzle on."[52] When a band or orchestra played, there might be several horns funneling the sound, but the singer then had to duck between the instrumental parts, with the band arranged in a circle around the horns. The whole process was exceedingly grueling, and involved continual tests and retakes. Perhaps most amazing of all was that in the early days there was limited duplication capability so that artists had to record the same song over and over. Each recording produced a unique product. For a singer, at most three horns could be used at a time, each horn leading to its own recording machine that had to be properly calibrated. A band could record in up to ten horns. So each cylinder sold to the public was actually a unique production.

Artists who were used to performing onstage for an audience had to learn a whole new way of practicing their craft. The opera singer Anna Case remembered, "You had to gauge your own distance from the horn for every note. At first, I was guided by a man holding my arm; if I was to get closer, he'd pull me closer, if further away, he'd pull me this way. Finally, I got so that I could do it myself, and I think I did all the acoustical records that way."[53] The Metropolitan Opera star soprano Rosa Ponselle considered the experience "dreadful! Of course I didn't know any better; neither did anyone else. It was all done acoustically in those days, singing into this awful horn. . . . If I sang too loud, it would blast, and the wax master disc would be ruined."[54] Edison complained, "When an extra-loud sound occurs in a song—you know, when an Eyetalian has suddenly fallen in love or somep'n—the recorder needle gives a jump, and then a tiny bit of the wax is chipped out; you can hardly see it without a microscope, but you hear it plenty afterwards."[55]

Recording was possibly even tougher for musicians. "It restricted your movements. You had to get very close to it, and it was awkward," Irving Kaufman remembered. "If you got a little too far away—just three or four or five inches too far—you didn't have quite enough presence. Now it was simple with the piano. It was an old upright, and they could just put the horn close to get it. But with the violin you had to lean into the horn."[56] Another noted that if he hit the horn accidentally, "that ended it—you had to make the record over."[57]

By the late 1890s, Edison could duplicate about twenty-five cylinders before the wax wore out, but artists still had to record numerous takes in order to create a marketable product.[58] Even after duplication processes were invented, artists would have to record a whole song perfectly—there were no overdubs or inserts. At the Edison studios, three master recordings were made, and Edison's team would choose the one they liked best. The recording process was grueling, and at Edison, exacting—"arduous and unromantic," as one observer described it.[59] They experimented with platforms at different heights for the musicians to sit on, arrayed around the horn. The recordist (they were not yet called sound engineers) moved the musicians around, testing each position in relation to the horn and to each other, trying again and again each time they recorded. The trumpeter Edna White remembered practicing all day, over and over, until her lips were so tired she could barely play. As they finally recorded at the end of the day, she missed one high note at the end of the song. After making two mistakes the next time through, she refused to play anymore. They had to bring the whole orchestra back the next morning, at considerable expense, to record the three masters of "The Debutante," each of which had to be technically and musically perfect.[60] Adding to the difficulty was the fact that Edison and his competitors were exceedingly cautious about revealing their techniques, so musicians were often not privy to the technical workings of the process: "How it was equipped and how it does its work are department secrets that even the artists are not permitted to know."[61] More than any of his competitors, Edison saw the challenges as technical rather than artistic.

In 1911 Edison rededicated his enterprise to the making of music, personally taking over as musical director of the whole business. He went about it in the typical Edison way—listening to all three thousand titles in the Edison catalog, as well as thousands more from the foreign catalogs and his competitors, taking notes on tones, techniques, and artists. Over the years, Edison worked daily and continuously on experiments to improve sound and tone. At one point he enlisted the pianist Ernest Stevens in a project to record every instrument from every spot in the studio. "On the floor we had marked seventy-five squares," Stevens recalled. "We'd make tests on each one of the seventy-five squares with each instrument—he'd listen to them and say, 'Assemble them all,' and we'd record the whole orchestra. He'd pick apart this, that, and the other thing, and we'd have to make *more* tests." Stevens began with the saxophonist playing on Square #1, and then moving on to each of the seventy-five squares. Each member of the orchestra took a turn working through the squares. Edison returned and listened to each recording, selecting the position that sounded best to him for each instrument.

> Maybe it would take four hours in the morning, because he couldn't give me any more time than that. Then he'd assign things. He might go over to the ice house, get a load of ice, and pack the horn. He would say, "Go through all those experiments again, and I'll listen to them. In the meantime, I'll take a nap." Then he'd say, "Go over and get a load of storage batteries, heat the horn, and make those same tests." And he had other tests. He was an experimenter from the word go. He said, "You know, Stevens, the biggest inventions come from the smallest things. There are always ten, a hundred different ways—better ways—to do just one little single thing." He was never satisfied with the way a job was being done. He'd think of so many ideas. When we experimented with sound effects, it was wonderful to watch his attention to the very smallest of details. He just seemed to have a scientific feeling toward everything: his home life, his music, everything.[62]

Because of this attention to detail, Edison's cylinders continued to lead the market in sound quality. When he came out with his first discs in 1912, they were universally praised for the superiority of their quality.

George Werner, left, and Fred C. Burt at Amberola recording session, Columbia Street Studio, West Orange, New Jersey, January 22, 1917. (Courtesy of Thomas Edison National Historical Park.)

   In 1915 the Edison company introduced a marketing scheme called Tone Tests, which invited audiences to compare the live voice with the recorded one. Edison summoned a distinguished group to the lab to listen to the latest model phonograph with a new sales technique. Next to the new phonograph was the illustrious soprano Anna Case, fresh off a stint at the Metropolitan Opera, singing alongside her latest recordings. As Case recalled, "Everybody, including myself, was astonished to find that it was impossible to distinguish between my own voice, and Mr. Edison's re-creation of it."[63] Then, Edison staged Tone Tests at the finest theaters and local dealers across the country. The historian Emily Thompson has observed that "the act of listening to reproductions was implicitly accepted as culturally equivalent to the act of listening to live performers. The establishment of this equivalence was no small accomplishment; for years, the reproduced melodies of the phonograph had been disparaged as 'canned music,' mechanically preserved products that had more in common with a tin of sardines than with

Home recording with Edison device. (Courtesy of Thomas Edison National Historical Park.)

live music. Tone Tests demonstrated, and perhaps helped bring about, a new willingness to accept these reproductions as an authentic aspect of musical culture."[64] And, perhaps, by this public gesture, the Tone Tests helped to privatize the creation of music scenes. From here onward one could listen to music—alone or with family and friends—in the comfort of home and be experiencing the real thing, not a reproduction of something else. The recording was now an authentic article, not simply a disorienting simulation.

Edison succeeded at his goal of producing the best sound quality on record, but he continued to lag in the marketplace. First, the new discs had to be played only on Edison machines, or with a cumbersome adapter. Even the process of production was exceedingly temperamental because the discs had to be created with perfect care. But more important, technical proficiency is only part of what makes for a good music listening experience. According to Stevens, "We had the best piano records on the market at that time from the standpoint of tone quality, especially the piano solos made at the Columbia Street studio in West Orange. That was where the side walls, the floors, and the ceiling were packed with cowhair." The packing was typical Edison genius, as he was concerned with controlling the movement of sound waves and the vibrations they made. After much experimentation, he settled on cowhair. Unfortunately, it was a technical solution that failed as music because "the Columbia Street studio had a dead sound. The moment you'd walk into the studio it would be so hard to breathe, because there'd be no vibration and hardly any air."[65] Similarly, based on his own reading of Hermann von Helmholz and the physics of sounds, and his own ideas about sounds becoming tangled up and crisscrossing in the horn, Edison designed extra large horns, including a 125-foot-long horn that went through the studio into an adjoining building where the recording machine was tended to by the sound man. The horn was made of solid brass, with 30,000 rivets; it measured 7 feet in diameter at the opening—large enough, it was hoped, to record a full orchestra—and tapered down as it passed through the wall of the studio into an adjoining building, down to 3 inches as it reached the recording machine.[66] He experimented with packing the horn with ice and with heating the horn.[67] The experiments did not work because Edison had some fundamental misconceptions about how sound worked.[68]

If Edison's ideas about sound waves were idiosyncratic, his music notions were downright limited and increasingly out of touch with the tastes of the public, even though he derived extraordinary pleasure from music. One of his musical directors remembered, "Music did much for Mr. Edison. It relaxed him and stimulated his imagination; he loved it dearly. Mr. Edison did much for music. Through his invention of the phonograph, musicians and music lovers in remote corners of the world were first given the opportunity of enjoying music properly presented by the world's leading artists."[69] George Lathrop noted in his 1890 visit how much Edison enjoyed music: "To relieve the strain of intent study and constant experiment, the inventor had just bought an organ; and, with the same energy that marks all his proceedings, he taught himself to play on it. He would rush out from his private laboratory into the main shop in the middle of the night, hammer out one or two tunes on the organ with almost ferocious vigor."[70]

Here, it might be useful to pause to remark on one well-known aspect of Edison's life: the man was deaf, having lost his hearing at age ten as a result of a bout of scarlet fever. How extraordinary it was that a deaf man was leading one of the major recording studios in the world. Stevens, who worked with Edison on a daily basis for years as his musical director, understood how

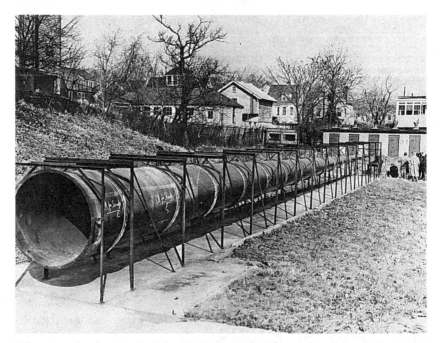

Edison's 125-foot horn at the Columbia Street Studio. Photo taken on November 20, 1942, on the occasion of its dismantling for the recycling of brass for the war effort.

Edison's deafness affected his musical acumen. "Even though he was stone deaf, I could play any note anywhere on the piano, and he could tell me the exact vibration," Stevens recalled. "Sometimes he'd get up and put his teeth over the rim of the piano, and get the conduction through his teeth. Of course the higher the pitches, why the fainter it would be to his ear. He could hear best right down the center of the piano, perhaps from two octaves below middle C to two octaves above middle C."[71] He despised excessive vibration, especially tremolo, and loved to point out to singers and musicians the etchings on the wax or the sound of the recording that proved what sometimes only he could hear.[72] Edison enjoyed telling the story of when he called attention to a wrong note played by the famous pianist Hans von Bülow: "'Impossible!' shouted von Bülow. 'It is impossible for the great von Bülow to make a mistake.' Well, we brought the wax over and put it on the phonograph. Von Bülow listened and, when he heard the mistake he had made, fainted dead away. I ran over, got some water and threw it in his face. When he came to, he looked bewildered, took his hat and walked out of the room—and I've never seen Hans von Bülow since that day."[73]

Adding to the hearing issues, and perhaps even more important, was the fact that Edison's tastes were pedestrian. He told his musical director, "Stevens, you know if you want to be successful in the sale of your records and be accepted, keep your arrangements simple and bring out the melody, because you're not making records for the musician, you're making records for the public, and the public likes to hear the melody not overly arranged. Play so they can follow the melody and detect it."[74] Only when Edison was out of town could Stevens record modern music. The chemist M. A. Rosanoff declared that Edison was not interested in culture at all, neither literature nor music: "If music is a language, it was Greek to Edison."[75]

Some of Edison's tastes seem to have derived from his hearing loss. "He liked low tones," Stevens recalled. "High tones, no. They seemed to grate [on] his ear and vibrate too much."[76] He disliked vibrations—hence the cowhair and 125-foot horn—so that the piano was really the only instrument that sounded good on Edison recordings. He especially hated the violin, particularly the E string, which he found irritating and "screechy."[77] "It grates upon my ears terribly," he complained.[78] He once mused about removing the scratching from the violin, not noting that the whole method of making sound with a bow on strings comes from that scratching.[79]

Victor Young, Edison's pianist and musical director in the 1920s, remembered:

I firmly believe that the greatest disappointment in the life of Thomas A. Edison was when his hearing failed to the extent that he could no longer enjoy music. From early youth his hearing was impaired but up until about six years ago he could listen to music by means of a device he used. This device was simple. It consisted of a medium sized horn from one of Mr. Edison's early cylinder amberola phonographs, with a piece of rubber connected to the small end of the horn and made to fit closely over his right ear. The large end of the horn was placed directly in the horn of one of his latest phonographs, when he listened to records. When he listened to the piano he would put the end of the horn directly inside the grand piano. His hearing with this device was extremely acute. He could hear "echoes" and "hammer strokes" which were at first indistinct to our normal ears. He would often smile and say, "It takes a deaf man to hear music."[80]

He sometimes judged the sound not by what he heard, but by what he saw on the cylinder or disc as the stylus cut a groove. At one point, Edison hired the violinist Samuel Gardner to make tone tests and to listen with Edison to other recordings made by the great musical artists of the day. Gardner remembers their session:

> He said, "Awful sound. Those people have a very shaky bow. They don't know how to draw the bow." And I thought, "That's very strange." . . . I knew immediately he didn't like the vibrato. So I drew a dead sound, the worst kind possible. He said, "That's great! That's great!" Then I found out that he didn't know anything about music. Nothing . . .

> He didn't like a groove that had a shake in it. So he made decisions not by the ear very much, because he was pretty deaf, but by looking at the record through a magnifying glass. He thought that vibrato was done with the right arm. It's done with the left hand! He said, "Now I want you to play that piece for me—give me a straight sound." Well, I played it. He thought it was marvelous, and I thought it was horrible.[81]

Gardner ended up playing with as little vibrato as possible and asked that his name not be put on the finished recording, concluding, "His deafness had nothing to do with his musicality, because he didn't have any."[82]

Victor Young remembered the daily grind of Edison's method with more equanimity:

> Mr. Edison personally listened to and "O.K.'d" every phonograph record produced by his company. For a long time he heard played or sung every composition desired for recording, and it was necessary to have his personal "O.K.," before recording was made. He was not a practical musician but read a great deal about music and had definite likes and dislikes as to composers and musical works. He did not like jazz; neither did he like the ultra modern compositions. He preferred compositions of straight flowing melodic outlines with not too complicated harmonic foundations. He seemingly never tired of listening to music. He would sit for many hours listening to me playing compositions, seeking to find numbers that met with his approval for phonograph recording. One day he listened for six hours without interruption.[83]

One imagines Young playing those six hours without daring to complain: "In working with Mr. Edison everybody concerned had to be 'on his toes,' so to speak. He had definite ideas and those ideas were carried out to the minutest detail by his associates."[84]

Edison's doggedness and perfectionism had built his career, so in music he continued to see all problems as technical. When Sergei Rachmaninoff— trained in the Moscow Conservatory, universally recognized as one of the era's geniuses as a composer and pianist—came to audition for Edison, he was summarily dismissed by the old man. Stevens remembered:

> There was an arrangement for Rachmaninoff to come in and play for Edison one day in 1919. Rachmaninoff came into the studio early, but before I could get to him to tell him not to play his Prelude in C-Sharp Minor—because I knew it would hurt the old gent's ears—why the old gent came shuffling in. He sat down in a chair alongside the piano, which was a nine-foot Lauter grand, and he put a special horn in his ear and said, "Go ahead" (*in nasal, high-pitched voice, imitating Edison*). So Rachmaninoff played the first notes of his C-Sharp Minor Prelude. The old gent said, "That's enough. Whoever told you you were a piano player? You're a pounder." Rachmaninoff never said a word. He got up from the piano bench, walked over to the hat rack, got his hat and coat, and walked out the door. The old gent turned to me and said, "Big head, big head."[85]

After initially rejecting Rachmaninoff, Edison was persuaded to have ten sides recorded for the label. After their success, Edison had no interest in more. Again, his stubbornness blocked him from sensing how the public was making use of recorded music. Stevens remembers, "He said that he didn't see why Anna Case and all the opera singers had to be paid so much money and bowed to, because all they had was just a little piece of muscle down there in their throat that vibrates. Everybody has one."[86] Ultimately, he did not see the point in paying the more famous artists the prices they were beginning to command. Generally, he would authorize a handful of sessions, enough to place the artist in the catalog. "We care nothing for the reputation of the artists singers or instrumentalists," Edison wrote. "All that we desire is that the voice shall be as perfect as possible."[87] He decided that while his competitors, particularly Victor with its Red Seal Records (see chapter 2), emphasized the names and celebrity of their recording artists, he would continue to market the Edison brand as a mark of the highest quality, eschewing the modern culture of celebrity and consumerism—or limiting the celebrity to his own image.

Edison had no shortage of confidence in his tastes, even in the face of rejection by the marketplace or disagreement from people with actual musical talent. "Mr. Edison was interested in musicians and liked to talk with them," Victor Young recalled. "Of all the musicians who visited Mr. Edison during the time I was associated with him, I think he enjoyed most the visit of Harold Bauer. Mr. Bauer seemed to measure up to Mr. Edison's idea of a well-rounded musician. He was perfectly at home in the mechanics of music (overtones, vibrations, hammer strokes, and so forth), and his visit seemed to end with a profound mutual admiration."[88] On the other hand, "I remember Carl Flesch's visit at the Laboratory. Mr. Flesch is one of the foremost violinists and pedagogues of our time. After it had been decided what new violin solos Mr. Flesch would record, Mr. Edison said, 'I would like to have you make over the *Ave Maria* leaving out the octaves. No violinist can play octaves in tune.' Unfortunately, Mr. Edison was right scientifically, but octaves played by Carl Flesch still sound mighty good to me."[89]

Edison stood at a divide in American culture that he helped create. He shared many sentiments with John Philip Sousa, one of his favorite musical artists, who had been the most famous and vocal opponent of the "Menace of Mechanical Music," as his 1906 article was titled, as a "substitute for human skill, intelligence, and soul." Just as the recorded music industry was reaching a critical point of maturity, Sousa sounded the alarm: "I foresee a marked deterioration in American music and musical taste, an interruption in the musical development of the country, and a host of other injuries to music in its artistic manifestations, by virtue—or rather by vice—of the multiplication of the various music-reproducing machines." Sousa feared the loss of that elusive "soul" in pursuit of mechanical, scientific perfection, declaring, "From the days when the mathematical and mechanical were paramount in music, the struggle has been bitter and incessant for the sway of the emotional and the soulful. And now, in this the twentieth century, come these talking and playing machines, and offer again to reduce the expression of music to a mathematical system of megaphones, wheels, cogs, disks, cylinders, and all manner of revolving things, which are as like real art as the marble statue of Eve is like her beautiful, living, breathing daughters." Just as the nightingale and thunder cannot be replaced by the penny whistle and the drummer, "the living, breathing example alone" can inspire. And Sousa rightly feared that the American working class would no longer learn to play "pianos, violins, guitars, mandolins, and banjos," but would become slaves to the commercial products and automatic machines. In the end, children, exposed only to mechanical music, would "become simply human phonographs—without soul or expression."[90]

By the time Edison met Sousa years later, in May 1923, recording technology was an accepted fact of the global soundscape. Sousa had recorded "Stars and Stripes Forever" for Edison in 1909. But the two men shared many sentiments about culture. Edison complained that "pianists pound until the instrument loses its character and becomes a roaring mass of conflicting vibrations which have no musical effect upon the audience—merely a confusion of sounds. I have keen sympathy for the elementally-minded man who longs for something he can comprehend."[91] Edison resisted the culture of celebrity and "fakery in music" and "fakery press agency work."[92] The historian Leonard DeGraaf has shown how Edison's dealers complained about the lack of "artists of reputation":

> Because of the difficulty of finding artists who could meet Edison's technical standards, the company tended to use the same artists repeatedly. As a result, Edison records not only lacked "star" appeal, they also lacked different musical styles and interpretations. Edison dealers understood that consumers wanted more than just technical perfection. According to one dealer, "it would seem to me that if your company would take on a new singer occasionally or a new orchestra, it would help matters. You must realize that the owner of an Edison instrument does not want all of his songs or, practically all of them, sung by the same singer."[93]

Like his friend and colleague Henry Ford, Edison straddled the modern world uncomfortably. No two men did more to usher in the twentieth century, yet both of them remained firmly rooted in their preindustrial roots.

Henry Ford vowed, "I will build a car for the great multitude. It will be large enough for the family, but small enough for the individual to run and care for. It will be constructed of the best materials, by the best men to be hired, after the simplest designs that modern engineering can devise. But it will be so low in price that no man making a good salary will be unable to own one—and enjoy with his family the blessing of hours of pleasure in God's great open spaces." This was truly a radical innovation for an industry still confined to the luxury market. As democratic and admirable as Ford's plan was, little did he realize how much his automobile would do to close up those open spaces. And when competition came from General Motors with different designs, styles, and colors, Ford responded, "Any customer can have a car painted any colour that he wants so long as it is black."[94] Although people revered the inventors, whom they considered heroes in their own lifetimes, customers wanted more than black, they wanted more than the Ford or Edison name as a mark of quality. In the world Edison and Ford created, the inventors and producers were themselves products to be marketed. The historian Lisa Gitelman observes:

> The connections between the laboratory and the marketplace were never more explicit than they were on Edison's product labels. Recognizing and encouraging the weight of his own celebrity as an inventor, Edison plastered himself and his lab all over the products he offered for sale. Records were "Made at the Edison Laboratory, Orange, New Jersey," a claim that elided existing corporate, personnel, and financial distinctions between Edison's experimental and commercial enterprises in West Orange. Records were presented as if they were the individual inventions of the lab, rather than the bulk products of the Edison Phonograph Works and the National Phonograph Company. The implication ill-served them later on, as market emphasis continued to shift from the novel to the fashionable, from the invented to the up-to-date, and Edison's cylinders started to look quaint rather than modern.[95]

The twentieth-century marketplace was fickle, demanding constant innovation, not just in technology, but in style. "By designing an entertainment phonograph and lowering the cost of machines and records in the 1890s Edison did much to create the phonograph industry, but he eventually failed because he based his marketing decisions on a set of ideas and assumptions that did not apply to a consumer market," DeGraaf notes. "Edison's ability to design efficient and reliable technologies served him well in his late 19th century producer market, but it was not enough to succeed in a market where consumers expected more than just technical perfection."[96] Edison actively resisted consumers' attempts to intervene. When he heard that users were speeding up their cylinders to make the songs more upbeat, he complained, "This change of speed is far worse than any loss due to having dance records too slow. . . . They are absolutely right time but young folks of the family want this fast time & like stunts & I dont want it & wont have it."[97] Similarly, Edison despised jazz and modernist music:

> All the world wants music; but it does not want Debussy; nor does it want complicated operatic arias. I know at my own expense. Sometimes out of four thousand records advertised all up and down the land, some made by men and women of very great reputation, the public deliberately selects for its own, some simple heartfelt melody, sung by some comparatively unknown singer, and demands this in such quantities that we have a hard time manufacturing enough. There is no closed corporation in music, no group controlling musical taste. The public wants what it wants; and it does not hesitate to let its wants be known. Why should it be forced to have complicated music when it cries to have simple music?[98]

But the public increasingly wanted more than the simple music of Edison's youth and imagination. As Rosanoff, the chemist who was hired to improve the wax formula used on cylinders, put it, "commercial demand was his measure of need." But, when Edison was told that the Europeans wanted grand opera and classical music, "he merely said, 'I don't believe it.'" Ultimately, Edison's tastes—and, thus, what he thought were the public's tastes—ran to the pedestrian: "His records in those days were mostly catchy tunes and plumber's family entertainment pieces in the vein of 'Mary, Gimme My Boots.'"[99] Edison insisted, "The public taken as a whole is very elementary, very primitive in its tastes. . . . My object is to reach the greater number of people with the most wholesome kind of appeal."[100]

Edison invented modernity but did not control it. The products he was selling were "Edison" and "inventions," and he had to let loose those inventions once they were removed from the lab to the marketplace. Although Edison partook of the cultural reconstruction of American society as much as anyone, it was that cultural reconstruction that rendered him obsolete. Soon, not the inventions and technology transformed the nation and the world, but the use to which they were put and the cultural transformations they ushered. Edison was old-fashioned, a relic of the nineteenth century, but also a victim of the increasingly fickle nature of the modern consumer culture he helped create.

2 · THE VICTOR TALKING MACHINE COMPANY AND THE SCENE AT HOME

At the Victor Talking Machine Company in Camden, New Jersey, the phonograph moved from being a scientific instrument to a musical one, inaugurating several developments in the history of the recording industry. Victor pioneered technologies in recording and playing and methods of presenting and marketing music to the public. If Edison's phonograph had introduced a new way for people to gather to make music—assembled around a cone in a cramped recording studio—it also created a modern way for people to gather to appreciate music, first in the arcades and eventually in the home. The Victor company eventually surpassed Edison in both, with a stable of recording artists and the invention and marketing of the Victrola for parlors across America. Although it is true that many people were involved in all the phonograph and recording work at the Edison company, it is impossible not to keep coming back to the man himself. The story of the Victor Talking Machine Company, on the other hand, involves a range of talented people who combined over the years to make the company a leader in the marketplace, establishing new types of scenes both in Camden, New Jersey, and in homes across America.

When Edison stopped work on the phonograph in 1878 to focus on the electric light, other inventors stepped into the breach. After winning the prestigious Volta Prize for the invention of the telephone, Alexander Graham

Bell and his partner Charles Sumner Tainter used the prize money to establish the Volta Laboratory in Washington, DC. Soon they patented a process for "cutting a sound line in a solid body"—recording onto wax—and developed the graphophone, a competitor to Edison's phonograph. In Washington also, the Columbia Phonograph Company peddled phonographs as dictating machines, but the technology was still so delicate as to be nearly useless. They began to use the machines to play songs at fairs and resorts, attaching ten tubes to each cylinder, collecting five cents from each customer.[1]

The first "coin-in-the-slot" machine appeared in a storefront in San Francisco in 1889 and customers flocked to the strange device that had tubes snaking out, which they pressed to their ears. The machines played cylinders by Edison, Columbia, and other burgeoning companies, including marches by John Philip Sousa and the popular whistling songs by John Y. Atlee and by George Washington Johnson, "the Whistling Coon."[2] When "coin-in-the-slot" arcade machines spread across the nation, there was an instant market for recorded musical entertainment. Columbia hired a hustling teenage piano player named Fred Gaisberg to find talent to accompany on recordings destined for the coin-operated machines to be installed at the Chicago World's Fair of 1893 and local saloons and beer gardens. Billed as "Professor Gaisberg," the sixteen-year-old accompanied dozens of singers on hundreds of recordings through the brief coin-in-the-slot craze of the mid-1890s, the first mass-produced recorded music in American history.[3]

The recorded musical cylinder sat at the center of the radical changes sweeping society at the end of the century. The 1890s have long been seen as a dramatic turning point in American history, what one historian calls the shift from a culture of production to a culture of consumption.[4] People navigated the generation-long transition from what we call Victorian to modern culture—all the dramatic, even radical, ways that American life was changed in the decades around the turn of the century, the changes that are hardly captured by the bland, textbook terms "industrialization," "urbanization," "immigration," "modernization," and so on. These transformations were felt as disruptions, no more so than in the 1890s, when the final battles of the Indian wars (and the "closing of the frontier"), the dramatic and violent battles between labor and capital (at Pullman and Homestead), constant racial pogroms and lynchings accompanying the disenfranchisement of African Americans, and the populist uprising and diffusion—all during a decade of "great depression"—culminating in the arrival of the United States on the global stage with the conquest of Hawaii and wars in Latin America and Asia.

Central to these transformations was the creation of mass production of goods and the commercialization and commodification of more and more of the stuff of everyday life, and thus of interactions and experiences. All those grand transformations were experienced on the level of the senses, particularly sight and sound. Similar changes were occurring throughout American culture, as the very dailiness of life for all classes of Americans and immigrants underwent dramatic transformations. So, for example, the halftone printing process brought color into people's homes in mass-produced, factory-made labels on the cans and boxes of new national branded goods. Kinetoscope parlors made available moving images from around the world. In the 1890s people listened to music in phonograph parlors and, increasingly, in the home. The types of music recorded "offered the same range and often the same names as a live concert or music hall show," but for people all over the country who could not make their way to Broadway or an urban vaudeville venue.[5] As David Laing has observed, "recorded music combined the polar opposites of the domestic interior and the vaudeville stage."[6]

The quality of the music recorded on cylinders was still, however, quite low, and the craze died off as soon as the novelty did. There was no way to reproduce the cylinders, so multiple machines with cones had to be set up, and each song had to be recorded over and over again. The cylinders were full of crackles and hisses, and the machines were guaranteed to break down regularly. Women's voices and violins were not captured well by the recorders, so the market was dominated by marching bands, whistling songs, and novelty songs with a piano accompaniment.[7]

A series of technical innovations would be required before the phonograph could be more than a novelty for music production and distribution. In 1887 the inventor Emile Berliner devised the gramophone, which played flat discs instead of cylinders, spurring Edison to renew his activity on the phonograph and release the "perfected phonograph" in 1888. Berliner's gramophone discs had the advantage that they could be mass reproduced from a master disc, thus enabling immediate widespread distribution. Berliner made an important connection when he met "Professor Gaisberg," the man who would become the recorded music industry's first talent scout, producer, and artists and repertoire (A&R) man, with a career spanning the next half century. Gaisberg had been working for Columbia Records, Edison's major competitor, when he encountered Berliner's new methods of recording: "Berliner placed a muzzle over [Billy] Golden's mouth and connected this up by a rubber hose to a diaphragm. I was at the piano, the sounding-board of which was also boxed up and connected to the diaphragm by a hose resembling an elephant's trunk. Berliner said, 'Are you ready?' and upon our answering 'Yes,' he began to crank like a barrel-organ, and said 'Go.'" Berliner's method of recording, with the stylus cutting a lateral groove on a flat disc, produced a "beautiful round tone" that left Gaisberg "spell-bound." "Before I departed that day, I exacted a promise from Berliner that he would let me work for him when his machine was ready for development."[8]

Major improvements were still needed, however. The discs themselves were unstable until Berliner contracted with the Duranoid Company of Newark, New Jersey, button manufacturers, to produce matrices made from a newly developed shellac mixture. Gaisberg remembered, "I was present when Berliner received the first package of gramophone records from the Duranoid Company. With trembling hands he placed the new disc on the reproducer and sounds of undreamed quality issued from the record . . . revealing tones hitherto mute to us. Berliner shouted with excitement and all of us . . . danced with joy around the machine."[9]

The machine, though, was not ready for market as long as it depended on a hand to crank the turntable at a steady pace. Gaisberg found an ad for the Camden machinist Eldridge Johnson's "clockwork motors" for sewing machines and commissioned him to come up with something for the gramophone. "Tall, lanky, stooping and taciturn, deliberate in his movements and always assuming a low voice with a Down-East Yankee drawl," Johnson was a typical, "independent, poverty-stricken inventor," toiling away as a mechanic, tinkerer, and inventor.[10] It was in his humble machine shop, tucked in back of Collings's horseless carriage factory on Front Street, that Camden, New Jersey's, contribution to music history began.[11] Johnson was unimpressed by the gramophone, but intrigued: "The little instrument was badly designed. It sounded like a partially-educated parrot with a sore throat and a cold in the head, but the little wheezy instrument caught my attention and held it fast and hard. I became interested in it as I had never been interested in anything before."[12] After a couple of false starts, Johnson was able to design a working spring-motor gramophone to take to market.[13] The company opened a small recording studio in Philadelphia and then another in New York City to churn out product for the first mass market in recorded music, and the machines (along with many of the records) themselves were made in Camden. Berliner's gramophone offered advantages, the most important was the flat disc process for mass duplication, something that was not possible with Edison's cylinders.

The Victor Talking Machine Company was incorporated in Camden in 1901, bringing together Berliner's and Johnson's work to manufacture and market the first lateral-cut, flat disc recording device and the discs to play on the gramophone. The company bought the rights to Francis Barraud's painting of a fox terrier listening to a phonograph, and had the original Edison machine painted over with the new gramophone. The image, dubbed "His Master's Voice," was to become perhaps the most successful corporate icon in marketing history. Johnson's machine shop in Camden became the home base for corporate and manufacturing purposes, growing from its back alley origins to cover acres of waterfront property.

From the start Victor was a globally oriented music business. Harry O. Sooy was hired in 1898 and later made chief recording engineer. Early on C. G. Child and Alfred Clark came in to oversee musical development, and Fred Gaisberg toured the world in the coming decades, establishing the recorded music business (like the simultaneously emerging world of cinema), as international in scope for production, distribution, and consumption. In 1907 Victor opened a recording studio at the Camden grounds, in a building on the corner of Front and Cooper Streets. Called Building No. 15, the facility was expanded numerous times over the years.

Berliner and Johnson's inventions, and the incorporation of Victor, revolutionized the recorded music business and the ways people could enjoy music. With Berliner's gramophone, the phonograph became what Jacques Attali calls an "instrument of sociality."[14] It also became an instrument of consumerism. Whereas Edison's original design combined recording and playback, so that owners could make their own recordings, with the gramophone the production and consumption of music took place in different spheres. Victor's gramophone, according to David Suisman, "introduced a structural and social division between making [a] recording and listening to it. With Edison's design, access to one assumed access to the other as well; sound recording was something people could *do*. With Berliner's design, a wedge was driven between production and consumption; sound recording was something people could *listen to*."[15] The phonograph went from the realm of science and invention to the realm of music and culture, as a "nascent cultural industry."[16]

The commercialization of recorded music changed the development of scenes in two ways. To a greater degree than they had with Edison, artists came to record *as artists* and, increasingly as *recording artists*. They gathered with like-minded musicians and producers to create recorded music as commodity, as art, and as disposable gimmick. It is important to note the ways these changes structured social relations at the time. Suisman notes, "At the turn of the twentieth century, a new musical culture emerged as the modern music industry took shape. This culture included many of the terms and conditions that structure the way we now understand and experience music, and its emergence had worldwide ramifications. The rise of music as big business was a multinational and transnational phenomenon, but one in which the United States had a leading position."[17] That is, these were not mere technological improvements. The phonograph launched the industries that—together with other industrial technologies—transformed the sound of America, creating the sound of modernity. "Music was now a presence in schools, in magazines, on the streets, and in commercial spaces as never before," Suisman observes. "Once the music industries were filling the air with music, American society sounded different than it had a generation earlier. Much of the change was attributable to the thunderous cacophony of mass industrialization and urbanization, but music mattered too."[18]

The turn of the century marked, as well, an extraordinary period of invention, intrigue, legal wrangling, and competition. Patent and copyright laws had yet to sort out the new technologies and the sound products they produced. The marketplace was a chaos of competing, often incompatible formats. As in so many wild-west–style new and unregulated markets, companies spied on, stole from, and sued each other. Emile Berliner was cheated by his own sales agent Frank Seamon and was for a while enjoined from selling his own products.[19] In the early days of the twentieth century, the main market for recorded music still consisted of nickelodeons. The technologies, both cylinder and disc, while improving, still provided sounds that were too jarring for the listener to get lost in. So recorded sound was still mainly a novelty.

Then came Caruso.[20] Enrico Caruso's 1902 recordings, made in Milan, catapulted Victor to the top of the industry alongside Edison and Columbia. The Victor flat disc passed Edison's cylinder, though it would take another decade for Edison to release his own discs. The sound was superior, and Caruso's rich mid-range tenor was perfect for the demands of the acoustic recording process. Caruso himself was already on the way to renown within the opera world, but the recordings established him as an international celebrity and recording star, perhaps the biggest star in the world.[21]

Caruso had already been a star in the opera world since his performance at the Lirico in 1898 and his tour of Rome, St. Petersburg, and Buenos Aires the following year. He sang, "as one of the good Lord's creatures in that happy land can—with the sun and the sky and the stars of the perfumed night in his voice expressing the ever-new marvels of the everlasting universal life."[22] After Caruso's debut at La Scala in 1901, the managing director remarked, "By God, if this young Neapolitan continues to sing like this, he will make the whole world talk about him."[23] As the Australian soprano Nellie Melba described, "As a voice—pure and simple—his was the most wonderful tenor I have ever heard. It rolled out like an organ. It had a magnificent ease, and a truly golden richness."[24] His voice was "described in every language with the same two adjectives: 'velvety' and 'golden.'"[25] When Gaisberg, then working for Victor as well as London's Gramophone and Typewriter Company, came to Milan to hear Caruso, he immediately knew that he had discovered gold.

Gaisberg liked to tell the story of how he telephoned the home office with a request to offer Caruso £100 for the recording of ten arias, and then ignored their rejection of the exorbitant sum.[26] So, the next day, April 11, 1902, Gaisberg set up shop in his suite at the Grand Hotel di Milano for a session, with the recording technology hidden behind a sheet hung as a curtain to protect the precious trade secrets of the gramophone. Gaisberg recounted the day in his memoirs: "One sunny afternoon, Caruso, debonair and fresh, sauntered into our studio and in exactly two hours sang ten arias to the piano accompaniment of Maestro Cottone. . . . Not one *stecca* [false note], blemish, or huskiness marred this feat."[27] Caruso's voice transcended the still considerable limits of the technology, as his "slightly baritonal quality helped drown out the surface noise inherent in the early discs, and his vocal timbre seemed particularly attuned to the characteristics of the acoustic recording diaphragm. 'He was,' Gaisberg says, 'the answer to a recording man's dream.' Even on the inadequate reproducers of the time, his records sounded rich and vibrant; and in addition they offered performances of surpassing beauty and artistic refinement."[28] By the time Caruso arrived in London for his first performances at Covent Garden the following month, the records had already transformed the world of recorded music, taking it from the slightly (or very) seedy penny arcades to the refined domestic spaces of the middle-class parlors. If the phonograph had brought modernity—with all its radical transformative properties—into the life of average people, Caruso, more than any other person, restored some of the refinement to the daily lives of the growing middle class. Caruso democratized opera, without removing its status as a mark of distinction, class, and refinement.[29]

It is important to pause on Caruso himself—the enormity of his talent, the effect he had on listeners, and the oversize personality that he projected, ideal for a celebrity in the modern age—prodigious in his appetites and grander than the rest of us, but humble, ordinary folk in his ways of relating to the masses and individuals. His son recalled, "The magic of my father's singing was inseparable from his person and personality. The combination of man and artist gave him the communicative powers that held his listeners spellbound; past and beyond the wondrous voice, this combination was the key to his enormous appeal."[30] Photographs record a man simultaneously goofy and personable, hamming it up in the New York City immigrant neighborhood on Rivington Street and mugging for the camera like a child, but more talented, and thus rightfully more wealthy and grand than we could ever realistically hope to be. But still we hope. Even his press agent, the pioneering Edward Bernays, could not resist his charms, writing in his memoirs, "His glamour affected me as it did others. I was talking to the sun god, and the sun god by his light obliterated his surroundings."[31] Touring with Caruso, Bernays recalled, "I felt as though I were walking on the boulevards of Paris with a popular monarch at the height of his glory."[32]

Fellow tenor, the Irishman John McCormack saw Caruso perform *La Boheme* at Covent Garden: "When I listened to the opening phrases of Puccini's music, sung by that indescribably glorious voice as Caruso alone could sing, my jaw dropped as though hung on a hinge. Such smoothness and purity of tone, and such quality; it was like a stream of liquid gold.... The sound of Caruso's voice that night lingered in my ears for months, and will doubtless linger there always. It will always be to me one of the memorable moments of my life." And, now, with Caruso's voice on record, the voice could linger for eternity. In 1903, when Caruso arrived in the United States to tour and record, opera became a popular entertainment for the first time, merging high and low culture.[33] Bernays, who made a career of manipulating public opinion and "engineering consent," concluded that Caruso's "publicity breakthrough hastened the acceptance and spread of classical music in all its forms. . . . A pioneer society had disregarded classical music, had felt it was enjoyed only by the highbrows and by those with special knowledge. Caruso changed this attitude, for he evoked in the listener a personal reaction of deep gratification that made his music universal in its appeal rather than limited to a special group."[34] Caruso—and Victor—democratized high culture.

Caruso became the face—and voice—of Victor. Compton Mackenzie, the great Scottish writer and critic, declared, "I do not hesitate to say that his master's voice heard by that fox-terrier was the voice of Caruso himself."[35] Caruso came to Victor's studios in Camden to record nearly two dozen times, including for his famous version of George M. Cohan's Great War song "Over There." His son accompanied him to one of his final sessions in Camden:

We drove to Camden in his powder-green Lancia, and I was surprised that he was no more apprehensive than any clerk or plumber on his way to work. He didn't talk much on the way, but when he did, it was obvious that he was not trying to spare his voice. Another thing I found amazing, not then but many years later: He did not warm up before the session, or at least I have absolutely no recollection that he did. He just turned toward the recording horn and sang. . . .

Father recorded multiple takes of a group of Italian songs. I had never before heard him sing at full voice at such close range. The sound that filled the studio was a marvel that finally made me sit up and respond to the miracle of Father's singing. He sang magnificently. The volume and beauty of his voice were overwhelming. The voice had such aural solidity that one felt the sound itself had a physical presence and could somehow be touched. I soon forgot all about the machinery, cutting needles and the rest, and listened to Father transfixed. . . .

It struck me that Father was not merely delivering a tune but was living each song. His face was animated, and he acted out the words as he would on the concert stage, so that I not only heard but also *saw* the song. The only particular number I remember was "A vuchella." He sang it several times, and each take was better than before. He had a good time singing it too: He would smile and pucker up—one could swear he actually saw some lovely girl smiling back at him from the recording horn—and he closed the song with a flirtatious wink. . . . The recording he made that day is one of my all-time favorites.

Fred Maisch, who was a recording engineer for the Victor Company for thirty-six years and who made thirty thousand master discs in his time, said in 1944 that when Caruso recorded the "Quartet" from Rigoletto, he had to stand

"back six feet from the other singers so as not to blast the recording apparatus."
Reading that comment and remembering the session of 1919, I am certain he
was not exaggerating.[36]

Caruso signed his first contract with Victor in 1904 and recorded exclusively
for the company throughout his life. He recorded dozens of best-selling sides
throughout his career, with some of his recordings unequaled to this day, his
final session taking place at Victor's Camden studios over three days in September 1920. His records sold continuously throughout his life and beyond,
thus "making a small fortune for Caruso and a large fortune for Victor."[37]

The force of Caruso's voice and personality made him a star, but the per-
sonnel and conditions created by the Victor Talking Machine Company made
his recordings state of the art. Working with the manager of the recording
laboratory Calvin Child and the artistic director Victor DeGogorza, Caruso
was able to sing with ease in the knowledge that the company would never
allow him to release a flawed recording. Calvin Child, in essence, became
Caruso's personal representative at Victor as the two worked closely together
at every stage of each recording.[38] And, alongside Nipper, Caruso became
the face of the Victor Talking Machine Company. Compton Mackenzie
summed up Caruso's significance for the medium of phonographic recording upon the tenor's death, "Fifteen years ago, when violin solos sounded like
bluebottles on a window pane, overtures like badly played mouth-organs,
chamber-music like amorous cats, brass bands like runaway steam-rollers,
and the piano like an old woman clicking her false teeth, Caruso's voice
proclaimed a millennium and preserved our faith."[39] If Caruso's singing
contained any faults, "they were the faults of superfluous energy, of superfluous emotion, of superfluous vitality."[40]

With Caruso, Victor began to pioneer ways of making an audience. If Edison had relied on his own image as the Wizard of Menlo Park to make the
case to listeners, Victor created a whole new corporate image that personal-
ized the relationship between the company, the products (both record player
and record), and the listener. With Nipper, the dog listening to "His Master's Voice," the company created one of the enduring advertising symbols
of the twentieth century. Victor also spent money on advertising as no company had before, taking out two-page spreads in popular magazines starting
with the *Saturday Evening Post*. Under Johnson, Victor hooked into the
already existing cultural status of opera to create an image of the company

"What a coincidence! That Caruso record you just played on the
Victrola was the same aria we heard him sing at the opera tonight!"

Hearing the world's greatest artists sing the arias you like best is an everyday pleasure
with a Victrola.

Just as real, just as enjoyable, in your own home as though you were hearing them
in the great opera houses and theatres of the world.

Hearing them at home on the Victrola has these advantages: You can make your choice
of artists and selections, and have as many encores as you desire.

Any Victor dealer in any city in the world will gladly play any music you wish to hear and
demonstrate the various styles of the Victor and Victrola—$10 to $250.

Victor Talking Machine Co., Camden, N. J., U. S. A.
Berliner Gramophone Co., Montreal, Canadian Distributors

New Victor Records demonstrated at all dealers on the 28th of each month.

The music world and the scene at home merge in this 1915 Victor ad in the *Saturday Evening Post.* "What a coincidence! That Caruso record you just played on the Victrola . . ." (Courtesy of the Hagley Museum and Library.)

and its music as "high class" by establishing the Red Seal line of records.[41] Its roster of Red Seal artists, including luminaries such as Adelina Patti and Nellie Melba, established its records as products of taste, worthy and essential for any listener hoping to achieve genteel, middle-class status. In this, its music helped create the space for "opera at home," establishing the parlor as a site of musical consumption and music scene production.[42]

The Red Seal line launched Victor to the top of the recorded music business. Even if the Red Seal line only accounted for a fraction of the sales, it solidified Victor's image, by allowing Victor into the sanctified space of the middle-class home. "The Victor strategy for selling opera records," the historian Marsha Siefert has shown, "domesticated opera's appeal and democratized its accessibility without destroying its value as a mark of 'distinction.'"[43] Further, as the historian Jacques Barzun long ago noted, "This mechanical civilization of ours has performed a miracle . . . it has, by mechanical means, brought back to life the whole repertory of Western music . . . it is like the Renaissance rediscovering the classics and holding them fast by means of the printing press. It marks an epoch in Western intellectual history."[44] Victor announced its strategy to its dealers in a full-page ad in the *Talking Machine World*, "There are four Victor pages in this issue. Three show pictures of operatic artists; one shows pictures of popular artists. Three to one—our business is just the other way, and more, too; but there is good advertising in Grand Opera. Are you getting your share?"[45]

The phonograph had already changed the way listeners engaged with music, removing the focal point of the performer onstage and leaving the static horn—"you can stare into a horn and know that at some vanishing point beyond the visible concavity there is something breathing."[46] When Victor introduced the Victrola in 1906, even that visual cue was removed, leaving only the sounds floating free in the domestic interior. The Victrola hid the horn inside Chippendale or Queen Anne–style cabinets, designed to create an air of class and elegance for the middle-class home. With the arrival especially of the Victrola, scenes could develop both in the small, enclosed enclaves of the living room and on a mass scale, countrywide as "affective alliances" formed across all borders. Historians note a replacement of amateur music making with the consumerist process of listening to a commodified product by collections of individual listeners.[47] These developments may stretch the meaning of the word "scene," but the most important factor to note is the change in the ways that people gathered to create and enjoy music.

Domestic spaces create scenes, too. Through the commercial distribution of sheet music and performances in homes, music creators and lovers in nineteenth-century Europe created a string chamber music scene that helped create the social and cultural dimensions of the bourgeoisie.[48] Chamber music "existed at the intersection of professional and amateur performance and of serious and recreational music making" taking place in "semiprivate" and "semipublic" spaces, such as at house parties and house concerts or exclusive clubs, fraternities, and rented spaces.[49] This merging of the public and private environments shaped the music, as composers wrote for this listening audience of critics and music lovers. Printed sheet music connected these communities across time and space.[50]

As early as the nineteenth century, even before the invention of the phonograph, "the basic practices associated with fandom—idealized connection with a star, strong feelings of memory and nostalgia, use of collecting to develop a sense of self, for example"—were present among music lovers.[51] The Swedish opera singer Jenny Lind was marketed by P. T. Barnum for her 1850–52 tour of the United States by emphasizing her personal qualities, and audiences connected to her in a deeply personal way. In the new world of commercialized leisure, they also felt the visceral rush of "the sheer novelty and power of auditory experience" shared with a mass of people.[52] These first music fans in the U.S. built activities to embed the music in their lives between the all-too-infrequent visiting performances by keeping diaries, staging amateur productions, collecting sheet music, and trying to catch glimpses of the stars outside of the performance. When the engagement of fans became too passionate and devoted for Victorian sensibilities, middle-class reformers introduced a new standard of "refinement" for music lovers: "ritualized, reverent, intellectual attention to the unfolding of a composition or work . . . removing the spontaneity and showmanship of live performance that might lead to obsession or spontaneous emotional display."[53] Many of the strategies of the audience-consumer—and the accompanying "moral panic" along class, gender, and generational lines—were already apparent by the mid-nineteenth century.

Sometimes the market and new technologies combined to create the possibility for a domestic scene. The phonograph created opportunities for solo, sexual, even masturbatory, pleasure that threatened the status quo—especially in the hands of women.[54] The main market for recordings and recording technology in the early decades was women, both for educational purposes for children and domestic spaces as a decorative object.[55] The technologies and the marketplace united women as consumers and active agents in the creation of the culture of modernity.

Early phonography advertising turned audio technology in the domestic space into a gendered means of connecting girls and women, as "the phonograph crossed the boundary between private and public life and in the

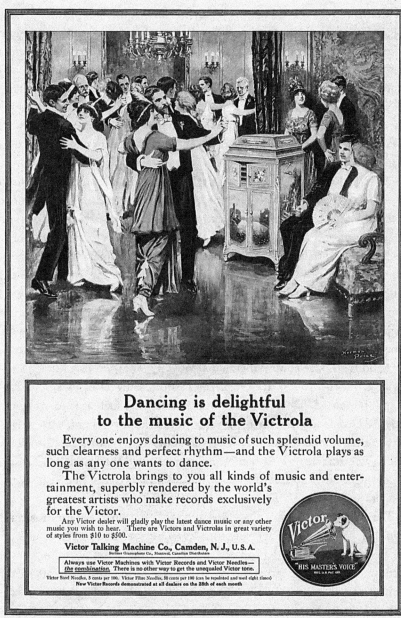
The music scene comes into the home in "Dancing is delightful to the music of the Victrola," a Victor ad in the *Ladies Home Journal*, June 1914. (Courtesy of the Hagley Museum and Library.)

process gave rise to public discourses that sought to negotiate this new relationship between mass entertainment and domestic space."[56] Home listeners were connected through "the illusion of presence" and what Simon Frith calls "the pleasure of familiarity," and, by popular discourses, women were assigned the central role in "negotiating the transition between mass-produced entertainment and the sanctity of the home, and mothers specifically were placed in the middle of the conflict."[57] For the middle-class home, the integration of mass culture into the domestic sphere was complete with the introduction of the Victrola, which changed the phonograph into a decorative item of furniture.[58]

With the Red Seal line and Victrola, Victor promoted itself as the bastion of elegance, style, civilization, and uplift for middle America, releasing a range of discs by the cream of opera and classical music as well as yearly books and catalogs. But, as its trade ad had said, the Red Seal records composed only a fraction of their sales.[59] Victor also released an extraordinarily wide range of popular and niche music, with artists of every type traveling from all over the country to record for Victor. Billy Murray became the best-selling singer of pop and novelty songs after he signed an exclusive contract with Victor in 1909. Other important singers included Ada Jones and Harry Macdonough. From its earliest days, Victor recorded African American artists, including the famous blackface duo Williams and Walker in 1901, the Fisk Jubilee Singers in Camden in 1909, the Tuskegee Institute Singers in 1914, and Paul Robeson in 1925.[60] Victor released what is called the first jazz record by the Original Dixieland Jass Band in 1917 and the first country record, Vernon Dalhart's "The Prisoner's Song / The Wreck of the Old 97," in 1924. The Victor Salon Orchestra, led by Nathaniel Shilkret, recorded thousands of sides in a staggering array of styles from dance music and jazz to the Red Seal staples of opera and classical.[61]

The company maintained studios in New York, especially for musicians who performed locally, but recorded from 1907 on at Building No. 15 in Camden, which was remodeled and expanded numerous times over the years to accommodate the increasing recording needs of the company. In 1918 Victor purchased the Camden Trinity Church building to record large vocal groups and orchestras, most notably the Philadelphia Symphony Orchestra conducted by Leopold Stowkowski.[62] The recording process was still exotic and mysterious enough that as late as 1918 Victor's Education Department could publish an extensive behind-the-scenes account:

In this 1922 Christmas season advertisement, Victor brings the whole world of music into your home with the purchase of the Victrola. "Christmas morning and in come the greatest artists!" (Courtesy of the Hagley Museum and Library.)

This article has been published in response to a great many requests from our readers, who want to know just what happens in the recording auditorium. If you yourself came to Camden to make a record your experience would be about as follows:

As you stepped from the elevator into the reception room, you would, first of all, feel the keen thrust of stage fright.

Musical tradition? The place fairly reeks with it. It isn't so much that you feel the presence of all the truly great artists of our generation. That, of course, goes without saying, but there's a slightly uncanny feeling. You can never quite forget that here, perched high on the banks of the Delaware, the soul of a singer is caught in some glorious moment of achievement and crystallized on a disc for the sake of all the world—the world of to-day and of all the successive tomorrows.

In due time you would find yourself confronting the horn in the recording auditorium, with a whole big orchestra grouped about you, but it would be arranged like no other orchestra you ever saw. Just what kind of a horn you would sing into, and just how or where the orchestra would be grouped, would depend a good deal on you and on what you were going to sing or play—anyway, you know, we can't tell too many tales out of school.

First, you would rehearse your song complete with the orchestra. Not once only, but two or three times, or even more, if necessary, to get your voice wholly en rapport with its orchestra accompaniment.

There would very likely be some shifting about of instruments or groups of instruments in the orchestra, and when the conductor was well satisfied you would sing into the horn a short test section of your song, with accompaniment. This is done to see that the desired effect is "registering"—and then you would be ready for the real ordeal.

The operator in the adjoining room would adjust the recording mechanisms, and from that moment there would be dead silence in the auditorium. You would watch the face of the operator looking at you through a tiny window—or you would watch for a flash from a tiny electric light. You might hear your own heart beat, but you would hear nothing else, till, at the signal, the down-sweep of the conductor's baton let loose the flood of sound.

Then you would sing, and you would try to sing as you never sang before, because you would know that not one audience alone, but all the world might hear your song.

The song finished, the same dead silence would grip the room again until the recording mechanism was stopped and the operator so informed you with

Victor Records acoustic recording session, Studio 1 on the seventh floor of Victor Building No. 15, 1925. (Courtesy of Mark Berresford Rare Records.)

a smile and a nod. And then, as you passed out of the auditorium, the orchestra might shower you with applause, or—it might not.[63]

The account failed to mention that everyday at closing time, the Victor Camden factory whistle would ring out, interrupting and ruining whatever recording was currently in process.[64]

A series of events in the 1920s contributed to the eventual end of the Victor Talking Machine Company. The acoustic era of sound recording for phonograph records was drawing to a close. First came the challenge from radio, which dampened record sales in the early 1920s. Families began to purchase radio receivers instead of phonographs, especially with the introduction of a product line from the Radio Corporation of America (RCA) in 1924. The following year, Victor signed a deal with RCA to include radio receivers in their Victrola cabinets, but the company could not compete in record sales with the free music offered over the radio.[65] The recording process underwent a revolutionary shift in 1925, as well, with the introduction of the new

Victor Records electric recording session, Studio 1 on the seventh floor of Victor Building No. 15, 1925. (Courtesy of Mark Berresford Rare Records.)

process of electrical recording. Victor signed a licensing deal with Western Electric, the Camden studios were converted to electrical recording, and the era of singing into a cone came to an abrupt end. Victor began to rerelease old records and rerecord old stars for its new line of "electrically recorded" "Orthophonic" recordings.

The company sought new lines of income and cast its talent search wider and wider. From the very beginning, record companies had searched high and low for any kind of music and talent that might turn a profit—aware that quality sells, but so does novelty. By the 1920s, the business was discovering many different types of music, but usually in niches—smaller market segments that occasionally served up a breakout hit. The birth of what we call country music occurred through the auspices of Victor records in the 1920s, with many of the key sessions taking place in Camden. The man most responsible, Ralph Peer, came from Okeh Records to Victor, where he became a pioneering A&R man, transforming the industry and the world of American music.

Ralph Peer was born in Independence, Missouri, in 1892 during that initial period of the explosion of popular culture and recorded music. His father worked as a salesman and machinist for the sewing machine and phonograph industries, eventually opening his own shop Peer Supply Company, which sold phonographs and the latest records. Ralph was exposed from an early age to both the recording business and the vibrant social world of the music halls in Independence and Kansas City, and eventually worked as a shipping clerk for Columbia Records as a teenager and settled into full-time employment in sales there after graduating from high school in 1909.[66] Traveling the Midwest for the next decade as a regional sales rep for Columbia, Peer learned the ropes of sales, marketing, and promotion from the ground up on the local level. After World War I, Peer joined the Okeh label of New York's Otto Heineman Phonograph Supply Company, and moved to East Orange, New Jersey, near the company's manufacturing plant, where he began to develop a catalog of American roots music. In 1920 Peer presided over "one of the milestone recordings and subsequent marketing breakthroughs in the history of American popular music": the 1920 release of "Crazy Blues" by Mamie Smith and Her Jazz Hounds—the record that launched a blues craze and proved there was a vast market for what came to be called "Race Records," music performed by and for African Americans.[67] At Okeh, Peer began to scour the country for regional music to bring to a larger record-buying audience, including a famous 1923 session in Atlanta where Fiddlin' John Carson's recordings launched the genre of hillbilly music.

When Victor Records pursued Peer, he responded with an offer that changed the economics of the recorded music business; instead of taking a salary, he offered to accept a percentage of the mechanical royalties, a portion of which he passed on to the artists. Peer understood that in a culture of celebrity, future profits derived from ownership of the rights to the songs, so he, in essence, set himself up as a personal management and publishing company, subcontracting to the label in his search for new talent and new songs.[68] And as he discovered talent in his travels across the country, he insisted they bring in their own songs, or traditionals that had been reworked enough to warrant a new copyright.

As Victor had created the first international recording celebrity in Caruso, Peer, too, looked for artists who had a personality that would transcend genre. He was hired to find hillbilly music, but he was always on the lookout for a breakthrough personality. He found one in Jimmie Rodgers, who, along with the Carter Family, emerged from obscurity with the famous Bristol Sessions of 1927, the recording sessions on the Tennessee-Virginia border that have been called the Big Bang of country music and, by Johnny Cash, "the single most important event in the history of country music." Setting up in an empty storefront on Bristol, Tennessee's main street, Peer recorded dozens of acts over a couple weeks, but Rodgers and the Carters brought something new. Peer recalled his own role in the transformation of the record business and its relationship with the public: "As a pioneer in this field, I perhaps set the pattern which has resulted in a really tremendous new section of the Amusement Industry. I quickly discovered that people buying records were *not* especially interested in hearing standard or folkloric music. What they wanted was something new—built along the same lines."[69] That line—"something new—built along the same lines"—captures the essence of the popular music marketplace and accounts for Peer's iconic status and success. As folklorists traveled the country and the world trying to capture the past before it slipped away under the onslaught of modernity—a task just as understandable, urgent, and valuable as any—Peer sought to make the old music new in order to reach a wide and widening audience.

If Caruso's recordings had made opera democratic, Peer's productions similarly broadened the appeal of what was previously regional and narrow. Although the categories of race and hillbilly segregated black and white music into market niches, they did not do so successfully. From the beginning the genres had crossed racial lines, for both musicians and audiences.

In 1929 Victor was bought out by the Radio Corporation of America. The company would continue to make records, often important ones, but now merely as a division in a multinational media conglomerate.

Victor had redefined ways that people could gather to appreciate music. Over the course of the nineteenth century, as capitalism and industrialization rewrote the rules of everyday life, the home became a refuge, the "haven in a heartless world" for the growing middle class. Within the home, culture and education became bulwarks against the corrosive values of the marketplace. Hymns and parlor songs were central to the idea of middle-class uplift, discipline, and the development of moral character, as families gathered around the piano, then the player piano and the phonograph. Red Seal records and the Victrola allowed middle-class families to appreciate beauty and the sacred as well as to interact with the modern world on their own terms. The phonograph became a piece of furniture designed to fit in with the other furnishings of the parlor, integrating the artifacts of mass culture into the home. Domestic space could be a safe place to invite the commercial world

Upon Caruso's death, Victor reminds the world that because of the Victrola, his voice will "live through all the ages." "Caruso Immortalized," 1921 ad in *National Geographic*. (Courtesy of the Hagley Museum and Library.)

in, and the other popular music of the period, from ragtime to jazz to hill-billy were just as likely to find an audience in the home. Public and private mixed in ways that created, simultaneously, family and community "scenes" of enjoyment of music on the personal level, and national "scenes" based on shared tastes and market niches.[70]

3 · JAZZ AT THE CLIFFSIDE

The Studios of Rudy Van Gelder

Hey Rudy, put this on the record—*all* of it.

—Miles Davis, Christmas Eve, 1954

In the years after World War II, a young generation of jazz musicians created new complex, up-tempo, and strangely syncopated sounds that came to be called bebop. Developed in late night jam sessions after the regular big-band gigs, this new music took the sound and style of jazz in new directions. Jazz had always provided the ideal setting for a music scene, and some of the best insights into the making of scenes come from the jazz world.

Music scenes evolve. Looking at how they change over time gives us a way to explore the relationships between the individual, the community, and the larger society. For example, the story of bebop is often told through the emergence of creative breakthroughs by a new breed of innovator. Bebop musicians began their careers as working musicians within a structured system that shaped the way they worked. The adoption of new forms of music making transformed social and business relations, not just their cultural output.[1] And that new form of music was not simply a result of "genius" or "inspiration," but also of economic and social forces that indirectly encouraged new forms of production and distribution of jazz.[2] Musical scenes are built on the intellectual and creative labor of writers, artists, performers, producers, engineers, inventors, and entrepreneurs, as well as fans, and that creativity is what brings everyone out and together.[3] As Howard Becker writes, "art worlds rather than artists make art."[4]

Bebop emerged from the "distinctively cloistered ambience" of late night jam sessions of musicians playing to jazz aficionados, who appreciated and purchased the music in the clubs and on the records.[5] This new small-combo jazz created a new aesthetic within the context of the structures of the jazz business. Various factors shaped bebop: small clubs that could not fit or pay the large orchestras, after-hours loosening of club rules, the opening up of the market for independent record companies after the end of the union ban on recording in 1943, and the racial inequality of the existing music industry also pushed young musicians toward the jam session for their artistic aspirations.[6] It was within these jam sessions, with their own codes, developed for very specific historical reasons, that a new music emerged.[7]

The jam session—what Ralph Ellison called "the jazzman's true academy"[8]—offers a type of subculture or scene, operating according to codes and rules that are opaque to the outsider, in an atmosphere that was never intended to be public.[9] Not all of what created a scene was based on a sense of community-as-unity, as jams were often competitive and hierarchical.[10] Clubs were nominally open to all, but resources, especially time, were finite, since even the long night contained only so many hours until dawn.[11] But as Scott DeVeaux remarks of a famous 1941 session at Minton's in New York that happened to be recorded, the interplay between the guitarist Charlie Christian and the drummer Kenny Clarke playing "Topsy": "This kind of telepathic empathy happens more often than one might think in jam sessions."[12]

These jam sessions provided the basis for jazz scenes centered in clubs in cities. The improvisational nature of the music made recording seem to be an afterthought, an inessential, possibly fruitless attempt to capture something that was an ephemeral, maybe even transcendent, experience. Just across the George Washington Bridge to New Jersey from upper Manhattan, an audio engineer created the space for a scene where jazz musicians came to unleash their most unrestrained performances to be captured for eternity. Although jazz is known as the most "live" of musical genres, Rudy Van Gelder's studio became a "holy site of jazz music" for jazz musicians from the 1950s into the twenty-first century.[13]

In 1946 Rudy Van Gelder created his first recording studio in his parents' house in the sleepy suburb of Hackensack. In fact, when his parents were designing the house on their newly purchased lot at 25 Prospect Avenue, Rudy intervened to persuade his father to include a sound booth off the living room where Rudy could install his first recording equipment. "The architect made the living room ceiling higher than the rest of the house, which created ideal acoustics for recording," Van Gelder remembered.[14] "When my father was having the blueprints done, I asked him if I could have a control room with a double glass window next to the living room. I wanted to perfect the techniques of contemporary music recording."[15]

After college, Rudy began a career as an optometrist, but spent every afternoon tinkering with technology and sounds in his home studio. Like Edison at his West Orange laboratory, Van Gelder took a technician's interest in the sounds, caring as much for the tools as the music. But unlike Edison, Van Gelder became the premier recording engineer of his era, capturing the sound of the new jazz as no one else could.[16] By the end of his life, he had recorded thousands of albums, many of the most famous in jazz history, and received all the major awards in his field, including a Trustees Award from the Grammys (National Academy of Recording Arts and Sciences) in 2012, honoring his lifetime contribution. The National Endowment for the Arts praised Van Gelder as "considered by many the greatest recording engineer in jazz" who "recorded practically every major jazz musician of the 1950s and 1960s."[17]

On afternoons, after leaving his optometry office in Teaneck, Van Gelder brought jazz musicians into his parents' living room while he experimented with recording techniques, microphones, and the new magnetic recording tape. "I was examining eyes on Monday and recording Miles Davis on Wednesday," Van Gelder claimed.[18]

Van Gelder's interest in recording developed early. At age seven, in 1931, he purchased, from the back of a comic book, a $2.98 "Home Recorder," a machine not all that far removed from the early cylinders of Edison and Victor, though it etched the sound into grooves on a plastic disc. "First of all, you got a 78 rpm record with blank grooves spiraling in towards the center," Van Gelder remembered.

> And then you put the disc on the turntable and then you put this device on top, which tracked the groove. And then along with that you get a little disc about four inches in diameter with a sort of a cardboard lacquer coating and there was a device that engraved a groove in that little disc. And you talked really loud like I'm doing now into the machine and you could hear yourself. I remember I put it up against a radio speaker, turned the radio up real loud, and sure enough I was recording music—$3 machine. That's how I started. (*chuckles*).

Soon, Van Gelder was ordering parts from radio suppliers to develop his own recording equipment.[19]

A fan of jazz since his youth, his interest was more in the sound itself.[20] Van Gelder had listened to jazz on the radio and visited clubs for performances, but his real love was the studio. "I was interested in music, but parallel to that when I was a young teenager I was also interested in ham radio. The technical part of that is building transmitters, receivers and audio amplifiers. It was my interest in music, as well as the technical aspects of radio, which brought me to sound recording," Van Gelder recalled.[21] On his trips to the clubs of New York City, he would also go downtown to buy electronic gear—mixers, amplifiers, microphones, and so on.

Visiting a radio station while attending college, "A powerful feeling swept over me. The music, the equipment's design, the seriousness of the place—I knew I wanted to spend my career in that type of environment . . . I loved the imposing look of the electronic equipment and how everything was meticulously set up. Radio equipment looks very serious. I also loved the equipment's design, which was modern and urgent. Back then the equipment's look reflected the excitement of music and the airwaves."[22] He clearly delighted in the design and formalism of the setting, but in pursuit of the same excitement that the musicians he was recording were creating with their tools.

He also understood how the technologies that were developing could better serve the musician and the listener—so that his studio became the node of intersection for the creative artist and the jazz fan who would ultimately purchase the vinyl product. "I was focused on making sure I got what producers needed," he told an interviewer. "The music wasn't top of mind. The technology and sound were."[23] His studio—built around his love of formal machine design—became the place where sounds were captured to nurture the human soul. As Van Gelder recalled, "My ambition from the start as a recording engineer was to capture and reproduce the music better than other engineers at the time. I was driven to make the music sound closer to the way it sounded in the studio. This was a constant struggle—to get electronics to accurately capture the human spirit."[24]

It is striking how even his technological perfectionism had an aesthetic dimension—his love of the machines was as much about the look and feel as the sound they captured and produced. He developed a reputation as prickly about his beloved instruments, wearing gloves and scolding anyone who dared touch a microphone.[25] But it was not merely a technician's perfectionism: "The microphones. I loved the way they looked. They were a symbol of everything I loved about recording studios. I loved all microphones. It was almost an obsession. When I'd see photos of jazz musicians recording or performing, I found myself looking at the mikes, not them. The microphone became everything for me."[26]

This love of the mics was motivated also by a driving ambition to capture what the human ear could hear but could not yet be faithfully produced on vinyl. The first barrier was the mics. "In those days—even into the 1950s—the quality of the equipment and records themselves couldn't keep up with what musicians were playing live," Van Gelder recalled. "I had to experiment to find the best way to set up musicians and microphones so the sound would be as warm and as realistic as possible."[27] Van Gelder was one of the first in the United States to use Neumann condenser microphones, which were much more sensitive than any previously available and created a warmer sound.[28]

Van Gelder was also one of the first engineers to experiment with the new magnetic tape produced by Ampex, switching from his early efforts recording direct to aluminum lacquer-coated discs (that were reproduced onto 78 rpm) for local musicians and singers. "Tape was more cost efficient and revolutionary for most engineers in the late '40s and early '50s," Van Gelder recalled. "It required a whole new series of techniques and disciplines as an engineer. I had always known what I wanted to hear, but the gear was too limited. With tape, I was able to move closer to my vision."[29]

Even the tape recording had its visual aesthetic for Van Gelder: "I felt it had a good chance of producing better results. And I fell in love with the design of the Ampex recorders. They were the most beautiful machines I had ever seen. Not a bolt or screw or anything visible. Just aluminum castings wrapped by stainless steel."[30] Van Gelder adopted tape even before Ampex had a service department, experimenting and developing his own "techniques and reflexes" as the machines were still inconsistent and unstable, even primitive.[31] Quickly, Van Gelder became proficient with the razor blade, splicing parts of two different takes together seamlessly.[32]

Even with its flaws, tape was ideally suited to the new jazz that was developing in the postwar years. "The beauty of tape is that it allowed for longer recording and mastering times. Three minutes had been the average duration of a 78-rpm recording. But a single reel of 15ips magnetic tape lasted 30 minutes.

Rudy Van Gelder at the Van Gelder Studio, Hackensack, New Jersey, in the mid-1950s. (Photo by Francis Wolff, courtesy of Mosaic Records.)

Tape also allowed for cost-efficient stop-and-start recording. Plus, we could splice out bad notes or performances and exchange them for better ones, doing rather extensive editing."[33] When record companies adopted the new 33 1/3 LP (long playing) record format in 1948, the new magnetic tape became essential for recording, especially when these new twelve-inch discs allowed for over twenty minutes per side.

In 1952 Van Gelder's studio came to the attention of the jazz world when Alfred Lion of Blue Note Records in New York heard a Van Gelder recording and asked his engineer to re-create the sound. Van Gelder remembered, "The guy told him he didn't know how, and urged Alfred to see the person who had recorded the originals. So he did."[34] Around the same time the owner of Prestige Records, Bob Weinstock, asked his staff producer and liner-note writer Ira Gitler to check out Van Gelder and his studio.[35] Other small jazz labels soon followed.

Van Gelder appreciated aligning himself with the upstart labels that were producing a new and challenging form of music. "During that time there were only three major record companies: RCA, Columbia and Decca," Van Gelder recalled. "Bob Weinstock, a music lover like myself, wanted to record albums that could compete sound-wise with the majors. I felt that now I had a mission: to allow small private labels to sound as good as the three big labels."[36]

Soon Blue Note, Prestige, Savoy, Impulse! and other labels began to book time at his studio. After the first Van Gelder-engineered albums on Blue Note came out—Gil Mellé's *New Faces, New Sounds* and the live *A Night at Birdland* by Art Blakey and the Jazz Messengers, demand for Van Gelder soared. "I was intensively organized, so I was able to engineer sessions comparatively faster than most other studios in New York," Van Gelder recalled. "I had to be organized—I continued to work as an optometrist throughout my recordings in the 1950s. The results of my sessions always sounded more distinct and dimensional than many other sessions being done then in New York, even in mono. . . . Recording was always on my mind. I would spend hours setting up for the next day's recording session, carefully placing the cables, microphones and chairs for the musicians. When the producer and musicians arrived, we would begin recording almost immediately."[37]

Continuing his work as an optometrist by day, and investing his income in new recording equipment, Van Gelder booked different labels for different nights of the week, experimenting and learning as he developed his techniques. "Alfred [Lion] was rigid about how he wanted Blue Note records to sound," Van Gelder recalled. "But Bob Weinstock of Prestige was more easygoing, so I'd experiment on his dates and use what I learned on the Blue Note sessions."[38]

Weinstock kept a standing Friday afternoon booking for Prestige sessions, and a "small motorcade would gather outside the Prestige office at 446 West 50th Street and travel over to Jersey"—often for lengthy jam sessions with minimal charts.[39] Alfred Lion put Van Gelder "on his team" and from then on Van Gelder had a steady stream of work.[40] The space became so iconic so quickly that in 1954 the pianist Thelonious Monk composed and recorded a tribute to Van Gelder's home studio, "Hackensack." Musicians enjoyed the experience of recording in the modified living room. "Musicians liked the intimacy of the relatively small space," notes the jazz historian

Dan Skea, "being physically close to one another helped the rhythm sections jell. At the same time, the warm, dry sound of the room made it easier to play in than some larger commercial spaces where reverberations bouncing off walls could disturb sonic cohesiveness."[41]

To accommodate the daily flow of traffic, his parents added a side entrance to the house, but otherwise accepted that their house was a recording studio by night, and "only once my mother left me a note asking me to do a better job tidying up."[42]

Van Gelder quickly established himself, by word of mouth, as someone with a unique ability to capture the sound of jazz in ways that no one else could—"techniques to reproduce jazz's salon intimacy on vinyl"—and his studio became a destination for jazz musicians establishing their legends.[43] Like Edison and others before him, he was a relentless experimenter, and as guarded with his discoveries, so that, to this day, many of his techniques remain secret.

As the jazz journalist Marc Myers notes, "Back when setting up microphones in recording studios was fairly standard and engineers were there merely to make sure everything was plugged in and that nothing went awry with equipment or recording levels, Rudy quickly became an improviser in his own right. For Rudy, microphones had distinct characteristics and properties, and when they were placed in unusual studio locations or wrapped in strange ways, they could produce a cozier, more realistic result."[44] Never part of the jazz tribe, Van Gelder ruled his space, wearing gloves to handle the microphones and not allowing anyone else to touch the equipment.[45]

The results were singular—each album "sounded rich in an organic, understated way, as if all of the musicians had recorded in a small storage closet lined with suede. None of the musicians sounded distant or faint, while session leaders were distinct but never sonically overwhelming."[46] Van Gelder was responsible for what would come to be known as the signature "Blue Note Sound." The New Yorker critic Richard Brody concluded, "He's not the only distinctive sound artist of modern jazz, but he's the one whose sound defines a sensibility and an era. It's hot and warm and also cool, but never cold."[47]

Van Gelder was notoriously circumspect about sharing any of his tools or techniques, refusing throughout his life to answer questions directly about his methods. As he himself understood, "No one else was producing those kinds of results on equipment that was available at the time."[48] It is not too much to claim that Van Gelder was a jazz artist.

The jazz critic Nate Chinen noted of Van Gelder, "So much of what he did was intangible. You hear it, you feel it, but his signature was etched in invisible ink. What is it, exactly, that you're listening for? Naturalism? Warmth? The sound of a room?"[49] Brody, in an assessment of Van Gelder's influence, concluded, Van Gelder's "own audacity fused with that of the artists at work to render the music with a sense of physical impact and deep psychological resonance. He approached technique with an artistic sensibility, even in its very inner-driven practicalities."[50] Brody captures both the delicacy and the power of Van Gelder's work as well as anyone:

> Van Gelder brings out the sharp edge of a horn's tone, a burr or a buzz or a glare, that retains the connection to the column of air from the musician's body, the pressure of the lips. His piano sound tends to the percussive, achieving a relatively thin but tactile plangency. And he's a master of letting the power of drums come through without overwhelming the texture of the ensemble. That's where the warmth and the cool come in: his live mixes capture a sense of the group— he lets each individual voice sound prominent while maintaining a sense of the musicians' proximity, of the intertwining of their sounds and, above all, of their sensibilities. . . . In Van Gelder's hands, even the most furious music maintains a refined clarity, a center of calm assurance amid the turbulence.[51]

What comes through from all the accolades is that the sound developed from a unique mixture of Van Gelder's personality, professionalism, and technique. Van Gelder paid particular attention to the placement of the microphones, developing different strategies for each instrument. For the piano, Billy Taylor helped him discover a method to capture the sound:

> I took some [Art] Tatum records out and some other piano records that I thought would help me explain what I was trying to get at. And we listened to them. He was the first engineer that I worked with who was that sensitive, and really just took time and cared about mike placement and all that sort of stuff. And I was just knocked out because here was a guy who was willing to take that kind of time on his own to listen and to, you know, say "Well, okay—play something." And I'd play something, and he'd put a mike in one place and go back in the other room. And then say, "Okay, let's try that again," and put a mike somewhere else. I mean, he was really just kind of making some comparisons and coming up with what he thought would get closest to what we were talking

about. And he actually captured the sound that I was looking for, and ultimately that seemed, to my ear, to be the basis of his piano sound.[52]

The musician Walter Becker claimed that he was always looking for the Van Gelder sound when recording his band Steely Dan: "The thing about Rudy's recording technique is how he got each instrument to sound intimate, with musicians playing close to the microphones. The way he recorded, you had the continuity of lines and the fatness of tone that made solos jump out. We wanted all of our recordings to sound that way."[53] Van Gelder himself spoke about what he was looking for. "When people talk about my albums, they often say the music has 'space.' I tried to reproduce a sense of space in the overall sound picture," Van Gelder once said. "I used specific microphones located in places that allowed the musicians to sound as though they were playing from different locations in the room, which in reality they were. This created a sensation of dimension and depth."[54]

This job was particularly difficult for jazz. With classical or popular music, the score dictates what will be played, so the engineer can plan ahead for changes in sound levels. It is not simply a matter of microphone placement. As the jazz historian Dan Skea points out, "Because improvisation is such an essential part of the art form" in jazz, "where the playing of soloists and the interaction of the rhythm section is spontaneously improvised, volume levels change dramatically and unpredictably with the emotion of the moment."[55] And each take was different.

Michael Cuscana, the jazz producer and leading discographer of Blue Note Records, concludes:

Rudy recorded at a very high level in terms of decibels, or dB. If you listen to a Rudy Van Gelder 1955 tape, he filled it with music. He was always on the verge of distorting, but he never did. If you listen to another '55 tape from Mercury or Columbia, you'll hear a lot of tape hiss because the engineers recorded at a cautious, lower level. Rudy got players like Art Blakey to sound like they did if you had heard them in a club.

He also had a way of capturing drums. Rudy engineered a McCoy Tyner record on Impulse called "Reaching Forth." If you put the record on and listen to it, you can hear every detail of Roy Haynes's drums, every piece of the drum kit. It's all just beautiful. If you open up the jacket in the album, there's a big picture of Roy Haynes and Henry Grimes in Rudy's studio. In front of the drum kit, there are just two mics on stands aimed at the level of the mounted tom-tom, and that's all he used. But he was able to capture all this stuff. How he did it, I don't know, but he just was the best at what he did.[56]

Each instrument provided special challenges for recording, but none more than drums. And Van Gelder was able to do something no one else could at the time. "Before Rudy, drums were mushy, pianos sounded dull, and the bass ... often missing in action," conclude the historians Jim Cogan and William Clark. "After Rudy, drums snapped and cymbals sizzled, pianos cooked and crackled, and the bass held the bottom like a swingin' ship's anchor. Modern jazz had a modern sound—and it was coming out of a living room in Hackensack.[57]

The drummer Kenny Clarke, recording with Tommy Flanagan (right), at the "Introducing Kenny Burrell" session, Van Gelder Studio, Hackensack, New Jersey, May 29, 1956. (Photo by Francis Wolff, courtesy of Mosaic Records.)

Van Gelder's skill was most famously captured in the "Blue Note Sound," but it is worth comparing Blue Note with Prestige to truly realize how Van Gelder contributed to the different sounds of modern jazz in the 1950s and 1960s. "Rudy had a good ear for jazz, you know, and a good feeling. He wasn't just a man who sat around the controls and looked at the needles," remembered Alfred Lion, Blue Note's founder.

> He listened, you know . . . every time I listened to the records from bigger companies, the drum sound was kind of pushed in the back. You didn't hear the details. And Rudy and I discussed it all the time, and I said, "I would like to hear the details, I'd like to hear the sock cymbal. You know, that . . . [snaps fingers] . . . and, cymbals on the top, and the ring. Really get this out, you know, and make it lively." Rudy mastered that after a while, and very well. And so we went from instrument to instrument—the bass—and we developed a sound which was the Blue Note sound. The records sound different from other people's.[58]

Lion recognized the unique value that Van Gelder brought: "Rudy's a very knowledgeable and soulful person. He's not like some—you know they call them 'needle noses'—they just look at the needle on the meter."[59] Lion was known to be exacting, but he also had complete faith in Van Gelder's abilities.

Van Gelder, characteristically, never claimed credit, always emphasizing Lion's role: "Alfred knew exactly what he wanted to hear. He communicated it to me and I got it for him technically. He was amazing in what he heard and how he would patiently draw it out of me. He gave me confidence and support in any situation."[60] Van Gelder was also careful to include Lion's partner Francis Wolff in the equation. Wolff's photographs are well-known, but Van Gelder also remembered him as "very much involved in the musical decisions at every session."[61] Lion valued Van Gelder's contribution from the beginning, telling *Audio* magazine in 1957, "Rudy is more than an ordinary engineer in that his knowledge of jazz, and the way he applies it to the recording of different musicians, puts him, to my mind, in the class of a creative artist."[62]

And, of course, it all came back to the two of them working together and with the musicians, as Van Gelder remembered of this work with Lion:

> He was unique at that time in that he had an idea; he pre-visualized or pre-oralized his records. He knew what he wanted before he came to the studio.

He had a good idea what a record should sound like, what he wanted it to sound like. He would then bring these musicians in, and I considered it was my job to make these people sound the way he thought they should sound. Now I wanna say, that's within the framework of the musicians themselves, too. Really, it's the way the musicians themselves felt that they wanted to sound. That's where it really begins. It's not with Alfred, it's not with any other producer."[63]

Bob Weinstock of Prestige Records took a far different approach to recording, but still found a home at Van Gelder studios. Living in Teaneck, one day he saw a sign for "Rudy Van Gelder, Optometrist." "I went in there and I said, 'Are you Rudy Van Gelder that does the Blue Note records?' 'Yeah, that's me.' And we talked, you know. And I asked, 'Are you allowed to do other people's records besides Blue Note's?' He said, 'Yeah, I'm not exclusive to them. I have time open.' And I booked a session with him. A Miles [Davis] session was the first one I did."[64] Weinstock famously had a laid-back demeanor and business approach. Bob Porter, the producer of Prestige Records, once quipped that the difference between Blue Note and Prestige was "two days of rehearsal."[65] And that was actually accurate, as Lion paid his musicians for rehearsals, and even included buffet and other professional accessories for the sessions. But Van Gelder objected to the characterization. "There are people who say that the difference between Blue Note and Prestige is rehearsal," Van Gelder complained. "That's just glib. That's bullshit. That's not even a fair way to put it. It resulted in a lot of my favorite recordings. You know, those Miles [Davis] Prestige things . . . they can't hurt those things. It's really one of the most gratifying things I've done, the fact that people can hear those. It's really good."[66]

Even though the procedure was different, Van Gelder approached every session with the same level of seriousness and creativity. Although the Blue Note sessions were more rigorous and exacting—and thus clearly significant to Van Gelder even at the time—"the Prestige recordings of Miles Davis, the Red Garland with Philly Joe Jones, the Jackie McLean and Art Taylor, the early Coltrane—sessions like that—turned out to be equally if not more important."[67]

The combination of the space and Rudy's meticulous attention to the process created an ambience in the room that led to unfettered performances for Prestige. In a posthumous appreciation of Van Gelder, the jazz critic Nate Chinen noted, "'Ready, Rudy?' was something jazz musicians routinely said from Mr. Van Gelder's studio floor, and the phrase became a kind of an in-joke, the title of a tune by Duke Pearson. Here, on the first track of 'Relaxin' With the Miles Davis Quintet,' we hear a less standard but more famous bit of studio chatter, as Davis rasps, 'I'll play it and tell you what it is later.' That offhandedness provides much of the charm of these sessions, for Prestige; Coltrane even begins his tenor-saxophone solo away from the microphone, as if stepping up to the plate."[68]

It is worth noting that key to all this—beyond the technologies and skills of Van Gelder as an engineer—was the unique atmosphere that he created in his home studio. "When they came to the Hackensack studio for a session, they felt appreciated, not merely tolerated," Dan Skea concluded. "Van Gelder spoke the jazz players' language and treated the music they created as high art."[69]

Van Gelder himself understood that though by temperament he was the very opposite of jazz musicians, he connected with them in some fundamental way. "I sort of had a rapport with the musician, and I tried to understand what they were trying to do. I always felt that jazz musicians should be treated in a way that was a little more as if it were a major effort than the way they had been treated in other places."[70] While musicians loved to tease and joke about how uptight Van Gelder could be about food in the studio and the absolute ban on smoking in the control room, they felt respected and welcome. The saxophonist Johnny Griffin recalled, "He'd say, 'Oh! Don't bring them hamburgers in my living room! Don't spill the drinks on the rug!' We'd drive him crazy—can you imagine all of us jazz musicians in his house?"[71] McCoy Tyner similarly remembers Van Gelder's fastidiousness, but understood, as well, that "he had things to do."[72] But Van Gelder appreciated the musicians: "I think I had a good rapport with all of them. They trusted me. And they still do. . . . Musicians would come to me, not all, but often enough that they'd say, 'That's just the way I want to sound' and believe me when they said that—and often—that stuck with me and I said, 'That's exactly—that's my goal.'"[73]

Perhaps the most famous Hackensack session occurred on Christmas Eve in 1954, when Miles Davis convened Milt Jackson on vibraphone, Thelonious Monk on piano, Percy Heath on bass, and Kenny Clarke on drums to record as the Modern Jazz Giants. The session was famous as much for its extraordinary product as for the friction between Davis and Monk, who had been included by Bob Weinstock against Davis's wishes, most particularly

Miles Davis recording at "Miles Davis Quartet" session, Van Gelder Studio, Hackensack, New Jersey, March 6, 1954. (Photo by Francis Wolff, courtesy of Mosaic Records.)

over whether Monk could continue playing his piano during Miles's trumpet solos.

Van Gelder had considerable experience recording these artists, especially Miles. It was Van Gelder who had first captured and created the recorded version of Davis, a "remote-sounding presence, with a modest amount of echo."[74] "Rudy had a way of capturing horns the way they sounded," said Michael Cuscuna, the reissue producer of numerous Van Gelder-engineered recordings. "He was committed to getting as close to the impact of a 'live' performance as possible in his studio—and he did it."[75] According to Skea, for Miles Davis's muted trumpet, Van Gelder was able to "record with a Telefunken microphone almost touching the metallic Harmon mute, thereby permitting Miles to achieve a great intensity without having to play at a high volume level. The piercing, icy-blue tone Davis was thus able to achieve became one of the trumpeter's trademarks."[76] The result is the Miles Davis that has been passed down to us—"a sound that transcends reality and the limits of quantum physics."[77]

The Modern Jazz Quartet had evolved from the Milt Jackson Quartet, and Jackson on the vibraphone with Heath on bass and Clarke on drums. All had recorded multiple sessions with Van Gelder. The drummer Kenny Clarke was such a regular that Van Gelder named his spot, right behind the keyboard of the piano, "Klook's Corner," after his nickname. "I benefited from his expertise," Van Gelder remembered. "He was so subtle, delicate, musical. He knew just how to hit the drums to make them sound beautiful and make life great for me."[78] As with Davis, Van Gelder was the first to bring Clarke's drums to life on record, capturing the cymbals cleanly and revealing the "intricacies of Clarke's best brush work."[79]

Christmas season was a good time for recording, as musicians were eager to gather the extra paydays. Apparently, however, Monk was not all that excited to be away from his family on this night. Monk had performed as a sideman, participating in the jam session environment, on numerous recordings at the studio. But he was not thrilled with once again being relegated to sideman status for a Prestige session. For his part, Davis had to be coerced into accepting Monk for the gig. Weinstock insisted, resisting Davis's resistance. While he had a famously laid-back attitude toward the sessions themselves, Weinstock was not without vision. It was not apathy that motivated Weinstock, but a different conception of how to draw the best performances. Originally he had no intention of including a Monk composition—the source of future royalties for the pianist—in the session. Only after Ira Gitler intervened did Weinstock agree to the inclusion of a tune by Monk, who was already well-established as a composer. According to the biographer Robin D. G. Kelley, Monk also carried into the session a touch of jealousy of Milt Jackson, another artist who seemed to be succeeding financially while Monk's career failed to take off. "So when Monk arrived at Van Gelder's studio around two in the afternoon," writes Kelley, "he was already a bit agitated."[80]

Beginning in mid-afternoon, the session stretched into the evening without much happening. Ira Gitler remembered that "things were not serene when I left towards the dinner hour . . . and not much had been accomplished."[81] A couple of solid takes of Jackson's "Bag's Groove" made it to tape, with the tension producing a Monk solo that the critic André Hodier described as "one of the purest moments of beauty in the history of jazz."[82] Following that, the group managed satisfactory takes of Monk's "Bemsha Swing" and Davis's own "Swing Spring."

Tensions came to a head during the first take of "The Man I Love." We hear it on the record. Jackson starts on the vibraphone. The playing stops. Monk says, "When am I supposed to come in, man?" One of the group is heard to interject, "Oh, no . . . Man, the cat's cuttin' hisself." Monk replies, "I wanna know when to come in, man. Can't I start too? Everybody else . . ." Davis shuts it down and starts it up: "Shh . . . Shh . . . Hey Rudy, put this on the record—ALL of it."[83] Jackson starts up again, and they launch into the number.

What followed was quickly blown into legend—with the most common tale involving fists flying. But no one at the scene confirms that. Years later, Van Gelder himself told the tale a couple of times, concluding, "It really wasn't a blow-up, just a simple incident."[84] It is clear that Davis asked Monk not to play—but to lay out—during his solo, and that Monk was none too pleased. Van Gelder recalled that some of the confusion came from the fact that the two musicians made differing requests to him. While he was adjusting equipment between rehearsal takes, Monk said to him, "Don't turn me down behind the trumpet solo." Van Gelder said, "Okay," and they continued to rehearse the piece.[85] Meanwhile, Miles had told Monk to lay out entirely during his solos.

Davis respected Monk's playing, but distrusted his ability to play behind horns. Miles said the pianist did not "push the rhythm section . . . I just told him to lay out when I was playing, because I wasn't comfortable with the way he voiced his changes . . . I wanted to hear the rhythm section stroll without a piano sound."[86]

There is no doubt that Monk behaved aggressively during the next take. After the opening melody, as Miles launched into his solo, Monk rose his full 6-foot, 3-inch frame from his piano and moved over to loom over Miles, who was hunched over his microphone. After the take, Miles asked, "What are you doing?" Monk replied, "Well, I don't have to sit down to lay out!"[87] All who tell the tale laugh at that line. In his autobiography, Davis recalls, "When I heard stories later saying that me and him was almost about to fight after I had him lay out while I was playing on 'Bags' Groove,' I was shocked, because Monk and I were, first, very close, and second, he was too big and strong for me to even be thinking about fighting. . . . All I did was tell him to lay out when I was playing. My asking him to lay out had something to do with music, not friendship. He used to tell cats to lay out himself."[88] Another time Davis emphasized that there was not even any argument, even after the brief exchange caught on tape at the beginning: "If I had ever said something about punching Monk out in front of his face . . . then somebody should have just come and got me and taken me to the madhouse, because Monk could have just picked my little ass up and thrown me through a wall."[89] Monk confirmed, with a chuckle, "Miles'd got killed if he hit me." And he later called all the tales of conflict "an invention . . . Miles and I didn't have an argument."[90]

Bob Weinstock confirmed: "People say there was an argument about Miles not wanting Monk to comp behind him. That's bullshit. Miles didn't want him to comp on one tune. There was no hostility, no fighting. I've heard that story many times but those guys had total respect for each other."[91] Van Gelder concluded that "Monk was planning something he wanted to play during the solo, and Miles had short-circuited his plan."[92] When Ira Gitler ran into Kenny Clarke at Minton's later that night and asked, "How did it go?" Clarke replied, "'Miles sure is a beautiful cat,' which was his way of saying that despite the obstacles[,] Miles had seen it through and produced something extraordinary and lasting."[93]

Although the legend disappears under even the slightest scrutiny, the music holds up. The tension was real. As Monk lamented, perhaps self-servingly, "The conditions were terrible. We were tired. The producer was not in the best of moods. It was Christmas Eve, and everyone wanted to go home."[94] But the products were the classic recordings released on disc as *Miles Davis and the Modern Jazz Giants* and *Bag's Groove*. "Miles credited it with pushing him further in the direction of utilizing space to 'breathe through the music,'" as one critic noted. "He called the record a classic, and said it's where 'I started to understand how to create space by leaving the piano out and just letting everybody stroll. I would extend and use that concept more later.'"[95]

In 1959, finally able to give up his optometry practice and devote himself to recording full-time, Van Gelder and his wife Elva decided to build their own house, and they designed a separate space on their Englewood Cliffs, New Jersey, property. Van Gelder remembered, "Back in the mid-1940s, Wright and his students had developed a concept of making beautiful homes from humble, natural materials that ordinary people could afford. These were called Usonian houses. We loved the concept, since a recording studio has to be an organic space. Cost and esthetics were important, too, of course."[96] Inspired by Usonian architecture, Rudy and Elva hired the architect David Henken (a student of Frank Lloyd Wright) and the developer Armand Giglio to build a studio on their newly purchased lot, detached from their home, in Englewood Cliffs.[97] The design of the rafters and arches—"bolted together at the top and joined at the bottom with a steel cable under the floor"— created the open space for a studio "unencumbered by columns."[98]

Van Gelder worked with Henken and Giglio to build a studio that fit his budget while creating the ideal recording environment. The masonry base was built out of custom-cast cinder blocks with the pigment embedded in the mix. The Douglas fir arches and rafters were uncoated, with cedar tongue-and-groove decking. Every detail was designed with the effect on recording in mind. And, typically for Van Gelder, he never revealed those details: "The way sound reflects off the masonry and wood is the secret. The five walls allow the sound to move up into the rafters and back down without being trapped or muffled."[99] Rudy Van Gelder paid attention to every detail: "Let me tell you, there's no paint on that ceiling. There's no varnish. That's the actual raw wood there the way it was all those years ago. They wanted to do something. They wanted to seal it. They wanted to cover it. I said, 'No, don't touch it. Just leave it the way it is.'"[100] The result was a "cathedral-like space" with a "vaulted ceiling made of laminated Douglas-fir arches and cedar planks, giving the room a Scandinavian feel."[101]

As Marc Myers describes his visit to the studio, "Snap your fingers or talk, and the sound appears to hang in the air momentarily, as if the rafters were evaluating the sonic quality before letting it go."[102] The jazz historian Ashley Kahn captures the dramatic effect the new space would have on the musicians who were used to the comfortable living room in Hackensack: "Upon entering the studio directly from the driveway, visitors were greeted to a surprise: a stunningly reverberant, atriumlike space, defined by two huge wooden arches intersecting far overhead. The pyramidal, ribbed ceiling— wooden slats neatly connecting the arches—leant the appearance of an inverted hull. . . . The studio radiated the feel of a small, modern-style church."[103] Some musicians resisted at first, but Van Gelder cautioned them to be patient, and once the first recordings were made—and heard—no complaints were heard again. The spaces were so completely different, yet nothing was lost in the transition as both rooms "had a live edge to them."[104]

Stanley Turrentine's "Blue Hour" session with The Three Sounds, Van Gelder Studio, Englewood Cliffs, New Jersey, December 12, 1960. (Photo by Francis Wolff, courtesy of Mosaic Records.)

Van Gelder himself had a singular personality, described variously as a "reclusive self-taught craftsman,"[105] (possibly unfairly) "an odd-duck audio goof,"[106] "fastidious" "meticulous"—some of these coming from afar, capturing his mystique maybe more than his personality, and not necessarily from those who knew him. "Rudy was basically gentle," Prestige's Ira Gitler remarked. "The only times I remember him becoming agitated were when people became careless with food or drink, particularly if anything was placed on the piano."

As both recording technology and modern jazz developed in the postwar era, Van Gelder pioneered their union—adapting new tools and techniques to capture the stylistic and creative explosion of the music in ways that other studios could not.[107] In contributing to the creation of the Blue Note Sound for the label, Van Gelder's recordings stood out for "their warmth, clarity, and sonic precision."[108] "Whereas earlier jazz recordings seemed to come at the listener from a distance," writes one jazz scholar, "Van Gelder found ways to approach and capture the music at closer range, and to more clearly convey jazz's characteristic sense of immediacy."[109]

Van Gelder was notoriously secretive about his techniques, but he emphasized the human dimension of his work: "All I can tell you is that when I achieved what I thought the musicians were trying to do, the sound sort of bloomed. When it's right, everything is beautiful. I was always searching for that point."[110] Van Gelder preferred not to reveal his secrets because, to him, the recording process was not about tools and techniques, but the people and their vision. "Usually my needs and wants are not related to the audiophile arena," Van Gelder claimed. "My needs are dictated by what the musicians want to do. They are interested in their own sound. I select components that facilitate that. That's what's happening."[111]

On recording perhaps his most famous contribution to jazz, Van Gelder remembered, "The most momentous recording of the 1960s for me was John Coltrane's *A Love Supreme*. It was hypnotic. It was exciting. It was different. But I didn't have those views when it was recorded." Typical for Van Gelder, at the time he was more involved in the process than the music itself. "You have to understand, I was busy making sure that the work was recorded perfectly. It wasn't until I was working on updating the original master [in 2002] that I listened intently to the music."[112] Another time he said, "The session was hypnotic, exciting and different. But I didn't realize that until I remastered the tapes many years later. When Coltrane was here, I was too worried about capturing the music."[113]

Praise of Van Gelder's work is not quite universal. Charles Mingus famously objected to the way "he tries to change people's tones. I've seen him do it; I've seen him do it. . . . That's why I never go to him; he ruined my bass sound."[114] After Van Gelder's death in 2016, occasional critics emerged.

Looking back on his career and what he had created in his two studios, Van Gelder reflected:

I've always worked for individual musicians and producers, along with labels. I still do. But I always try to work for the little guy and make it possible for him to compete with the big guys—technically and musically. That's the way I also handled my business. I could have expanded, hiring lots of people. But I decided to stay small. . . . Sometimes I sit here and think of all the great artists who came through and all the music that was made here. The musicians are still alive in my mind, just like the last time I saw them here."[115]

Despite his technical bent—the fact that he looked like the engineer he was—he took an artist's view of his own role in the process. In a 2008 interview with the National Endowment for the Arts, Van Gelder said:

Jazz essentially is improvised, so to sit there and listen to a musician improvising with a band and everyone playing together, hopefully that creates an atmosphere that can never be reproduced because you're there at the presence of the creation of the music. . . . So what I do is I endeavor to reproduce that moment and make sure that what they're trying to say is presented in the best possible way. The essential thing that's missing is the improvisation part. I don't consider that I have a sound. I'm not the performer. . . . It's my job to make sure that I understand what he's trying to do and present it in an environment that he's comfortable in and then deliver that for the producer who's hiring me.[116]

4 · TRANSYLVANIA BANDSTAND AND ROCKIN' WITH THE COOL GHOUL

In the mid-1960s, at the height of American youth's post Beatle-mania obsession with rock 'n' roll, New Jersey teenagers gathered daily around their television sets to rock along with *Disc-O-Teen*, a live-in-studio pop music show hosted by Zacherley, the pioneering horror TV host. It is easy to under-estimate the revolutionary influence of the arrival of the Beatles in 1964. It all seems so quaint and even cute in retrospect and in comparison to what we now know was to come in the following years. But, as much as any single event, the Beatles appearances on the *Ed Sullivan Show* for three consecu-tive weeks, coming so soon after the assassination of President John F. Ken-nedy, unleashed a social revolution. Sure, the foundations were there. JFK had already asked young people what they could do for their country, the Stu-dents for a Democratic Society had already called on youth to reclaim the American dream, Freedom Riders had already desegregated buses and lunch counters, and Bob Dylan had just announced to young America that "The Times They Are a-Changin.'" But the Beatles unleashed the ids of millions of kids, giving them the freedom to create their own identities and a new sense of what was possible, both individually and communally.

Premiering in Newark, New Jersey, in May 1965, *Disc-O-Teen* followed the formula that *American Bandstand* had perfected over the past decade of rock bands promoting their current hits surrounded by enthusiastically dancing teens, but with a twist. The central character on *Disc-O-Teen* was Zacherley, the man Dick Clark dubbed the Cool Ghoul.[1] Appearing onstage in an undertaker's costume, his face blacked up, intoning the band introductions and between-song patter in his trademark spectral voice, Zacherley, even more than the dancers or the bands, gave the show its character.

John Zacherle began his career in show business in 1957 with the character of Roland, a vampiric television host in Philadelphia. Roland introduced the *Million Dollar Movie Shock Theater* showings of the old horror films from the 1930s and 1940s, cutting in during commercial breaks to perform "experiments" in his laboratory with his wife (always unseen from inside her coffin) and his lab assistant Gasport. After developing a following in Philly, Zacherle was lured to New York to host *Chiller Theatre* in 1961 where he became Zacherley. Universal Studios had released its vault of old horror films to television, and there was a whole new generation of kids ready to be scared sleepless by Boris Karloff, Lon Chaney, and "TV's Loveable Ghoul."[2]

The character of Zacherley was a true original, both scary and funny, "a cadaverous undertaker with hollowed cheeks, white pasty skin, hair parted in the middle like Alfalfa and a delicious and droll delivery that signaled to every kid watching that this indeed was where the underground army would truly begin."[3] Kids and teens struggled to stay awake, or sneaked back to the living room to watch after their parents had gone to bed, to catch Zach's antics, as he broke into the movies to engage in dialogue with the characters or conduct an experiment on a brain (made out of cauliflower and Jell-O). The guitarist Steven Van Zandt, who became a fan growing up in Middletown Township, remembers, "Zacherley would come into the middle of the monster movie and suddenly appear doing something hilarious, and it was great— he had a great show. He'd have that laboratory going on, and he'd do some bits there and in the middle of the movie he'd show up dancing with a gorilla—it was hilarious."[4]

Zacherley developed a rabid cult following of young viewers who would watch alone at night, then eagerly meet up with their friends at school the next day to compare notes on Zach and see who had managed to stay up the latest. Although Zacherley's shtick seems so corny now (and it was even then), he also understood how to use the medium to build suspense and scare the viewer, especially young viewers, up late, watching the old horror films alone. The show was canceled in 1963, but Zach had made an indelible impression on youngsters in the New York area. One fan remembers,

"Zacherley was forbidden. He was every parent's nightmare, appearing on late night TV—on school nights!—and enlisting a growing army of young lab assistants in the eternal struggle to stay up as late as possible."[5]

A couple of years later, a group of television producers was planning to launch a new channel way out on the fringes of the broadcast medium on UHF, the ultra-high frequency channels above Channel 13 on the television dial. They were looking to create counterprogramming to lure viewers away from the handful of national networks and local stations, and they wanted to do it cheaply. UHF was out of the way for most viewers, but kids would go there if the programming existed. For one of the financiers, the motive was to sell UHF set-top converters, as older sets were not equipped to find the signal.[6] The writer Barry Landers approached the program director Fred Sayles for a job at the new station and together they came up with the idea for a teen dance show; Sayles suggested Zacherley.

WNJU TV-47 launched on May 16, 1965, with Sayles and Zacherley replacing the test pattern at 9:00 P.M. to introduce the station's new shows, which included a kids' show and professional wrestling. Part of the wave of local dance shows after the success of *American Bandstand*, *Disc-O-Teen* broadcast live every weekday at 6:00 P.M. (with a taped show on Saturdays) from the 10,000-square-foot Studio A—"the largest TV studio of any independent TV station in the entire USA"—on the second floor of the Mosque Theatre (also known as Symphony Hall) in Newark, an impressive, if well-worn, neoclassical edifice, originally opened as a Masonic temple in 1925, with imposing ionic columns and a glass dome over the sidewalk.[7]

On *Disc-O-Teen* kids danced to the latest popular recorded music or live local bands. Barry Landers, who became the show's producer, remembered, "We would ask the kids what the hit records were, and we went out and bought them. . . . We had no concept at all as to what was a hit. . . . They choreographed a lot of the dances."[8] Too poor to pay the fees for professional bands to play live, or even lip-synch, the show instead mixed visits from touring bands who chatted with Zach and judged dance contests. Local bands played covers of the latest hits live in the show's Battle of the Bands. As one regular described the scene, kids would "frug/jerk/monkey/swim/twist to canned music until the band would make its appearance, perform two songs live, after which they'd pony/stroll/stomp/watusi to a few more songs. Zach would talk to the band and some lucky audience members, do a live commercial or two, say 'Goodnight, whatever you are!' and fade to black."[9]

Disc-O-Teen created the environment for the formation of a scene, with dancing on the show as a social act and participation in a musical community.[10] Through this scene teenagers developed a sense of themselves as active participants in the creation of their own lives and community.[11] The community was not only local, based at the show, but generational and translocal, as young people connected to others through the burgeoning national (and global) taste-based youth culture of the era.[12]

Youth culture has been a useful category of historical analysis, and, although not all the scenes in this book are made up of young people, some are fruitfully examined through the history of youth culture, especially the communities and geographies of youth, the spaces that young people inhabit individually and in groups. Youth culture scenes are always hybrid, neither fully autonomous nor fully determined by outside sources such as parents or mass culture.[13] The teen dance show was one such space, where young people carved out terrain to identify insiders and outsiders—with locally specific rules—and to situate themselves within the larger world of youth culture and society at large. The environs of the show provided a place for ritual, custom, history, creativity, consumption, pleasure, stimulation, danger, escape, and "the release of deep seated emotions and desires in close proximity to others."[14]

Sometimes the involvement of scenesters can be viewed as a type of tribalism, almost communal, though not without stratification.[15] Scenes are often (though not always) democratic, where engagement becomes a kind of "participatory performance" where everyone is simultaneously the performer and the audience.[16] The scene at *Disc-O-Teen* is a prime example of the "grassroots networks and activities" that constitute music worlds.[17] It is a useful place to track the "micro-mobilization" and networks in showing how local scenes are connected to others and to larger worlds of meaning, in making "music as collective action."[18]

From the beginning of the show, a regular group of dancers appeared, many coming every day from the surrounding neighborhoods and suburbs. Many kids came from the Newark high schools—Arts, East Side, and especially Barringer—walking up Broad Street or taking the bus after school. But others came by bus, train, or parents' car from all over the region, from Maplewood to Teaneck, Kenilworth, and Springfield, Irvington, Keyport, Hillside, Elizabeth, and South Plainfield. Some even came from New York, with a contingent regularly traveling in from Staten Island: "It was a long trip from S.I. and we had to convince someone's father to drive us there or make the trek to Manhattan (by Ferry!), where we could get the Path train to Newark and then walk to The Mosque Theater. The whole trip could take up to 2 hours one way and we would have to bolt out of school so we could get there on time."[19] One boy frequently made the two-hour journey by subway and bus from the Bronx to appear on "DOT," as they called it.

Good dancers were invited back and given monthly passes. Unlike on *American Bandstand*, the dancers did not have to come as couples, so girls predominated. Though the minimum age was supposed to be sixteen, kids as young as twelve made themselves up to look older to get in. The regulars developed a familiarity and camaraderie from their experience on the show. Zacherley was the star, but the kids made the show, even adding their own artwork to the set, especially one regular's large horror movie character posters.[20] The show helped some of the kids to forge a new identity. "I didn't really fit in at high school," one regular remembered, "but when I walked into that studio, all of a sudden it clicked. There were a hundred or so people in there just like me, and they became my peer group."[21] Another girl knew she had found her place in the world when she discovered the show:

> I was playing around with my parent's tv set and somehow switched to the UHF band. What a delightful sight met my eyes when I saw kids dancing on a show that was being taped not far from where I lived. I immediately sent away for tickets and ran out to buy something groovey to wear. With my best friend Chrissie in tow, we found ourselves at The Mosque Theater in Newark dancing under the hottest lights ever! As we waited to tape a second show lined up in the hallway, Barry Landers approached us and asked if we'd like to be regulars on the show. Coming from high schools where we were dubbed Beatle Beatle Rolling Stone, had stones thrown at us and were truly the outcasts, this sounded like a great idea to us.[22]

Cliques, crushes, romances, best-friends-for-life—the typical fare of teens—developed on the set. Some kids came in groups, secure in their in-crowd status. Others came alone and never felt quite accepted.[23] Some individuals earned nicknames. So Carol became Donut Girl because she brought donuts in from her job at a bakery.[24] Marsha became Flower Girl.[25] Linda P.— "the beauty who stole many a male viewer's heart"—was universally adored by the boys on set and watching at home.[26] The camera men favored the prettier girls and better dancers, including Heather, who would sneak away from rehearsals at the Newark Ballet company and, at "barely 80 pounds and under five foot . . . got a lot of camera time."[27]

Several of the girls designed and made their own clothes, often in the hours just before the show, influenced by the London scene through listening to records and reading *Rave Magazine*.[28] Chris D. developed a distinctive and recognizable style, featuring bull's-eye tops, silver miniskirts or pants, mod boots, thick black hair and "unique, geometric op-art clothing—a graphic look that really stood out on B+W TV."[29]

The clothes were an essential part of creating community and identity through the show. One male regular remembers:

> Wearing the most impractical outfits on DOT because they were cool looking. I can remember walking around in the middle of the dog days of August dressed in a full length dress military coat (wool) with long sleeves and also military jackets from West Point in the dead of Summer. I remember neighbor's [*sic*] of ours trying to be "helpful" to my parents by alerting my mom that it was typical "junkie" behavior to wear long sleeves even in the Summertime. I remember on days that my Dad would drive us to DOT that the neighbors would actually come out of their houses and stand on their lawns to watch Claudia, Jill, Russ and Janet Powell, and Rick arrive at my house in their mini dresses and Mod regalia. It's really funny to think back at how outrageous that all was regarded back then, but I also remember at the time that it felt really rebellious and almost a little dangerous.[30]

Regulars hung out at Nick's, the greasy-spoon diner on Broad Street across from the Mosque Theater. In the summer they met for ice cream and gossip; in the winter Nick's provided the warmth not available for those waiting under the marquee for Joe the Cop to let them in. The waitress adored the kids, despite their low tips and typical teenage pranks with salt and sugar shakers.[31] When a group of *Disc-O-Teen* regulars pulled pranks on the set, one time covering the ladies room with toilet paper and drawing on the mirrors with lipstick and soap, they incurred the wrath of the show's producer, Barry Landers, who threatened them with banishment from the show.[32]

The regulars developed their own slang and in-group symbols. In the summer of 1966, dancers on the show began to flash the V sign, which they called Crunch, to each other and the camera, as a signal of "solidarity for those who danced on the show."[33] While the V sign had meant "Victory" during World War II, and was coming to be used as a symbol of peace to young people across the country, on *Disc-O-Teen* Crunch had a decidedly sexual connotation, a "secret symbol for sex, sexiness—or an exceptionally large part of the male anatomy."[34] As one regular remembered, "It became like a communication code between Discoteen regulars with almost a rebellious implication, as we enjoyed the fact that most adults and outsiders had a totally different interpretation of it's [*sic*] meaning. After it became a common symbol for the peace movement in 1967, most people assumed we were all just promoting peace, which made it more fun for us to do."[35] Although there were plenty of male regulars, clearly the girls dominated the scene, drawing the attention of the cameramen and the audience. It is striking how dominant the girls were in the scene. As with other fan communities, the *Disc-O-Teen* environment provided a space for teenage girls to navigate adolescence and the wider world of mass culture, straddling the line of consumer and producer within the subcultural community.[36]

The bands, on the other hand, were almost 100 percent male. *Disc-O-Teen* featured, in addition to the regular dancers, local garage bands stocked from the local high schools and junior high schools. Among the local bands to appear on the show were: the Newbreed, the Splynters (with the lead singer pushed around the set in a coffin),[37] the Gingermen, Chips & Co., the Fugitives, Carnival of Souls, Four Roses, Gyrations, Secret Seven, Danny and Diego, the Critters, the Fugitives, Broken Bones, Gilgos 5, Every Mother's Son, the Strays, the Mark V, Confederate Society, Holy Droners, Herald Square, and the Doughboys.[38] Others included the Explorers, the Henchmen, the Deep End, the Primates, the Luvs, Vito and the Overtones, the Eight Feet (four girls), Johnny and the High Keys, the Artie Ehman Trio (featuring a blind drummer), the Corvairs, Donny Vann, Gayle Hanness, Scott Fagan, the Ascots who became the Doughboys. Most played covers of hits by the Rolling Stones and other British bands, though some played original compositions.

Richard X. Heymann recalls the appearance of the Ascots:

You see, the day of the show, "Paint It Black" by the Rolling Stones hit the shelves of Gregory's Music Store in Plainfield and our guitarist Willy was there to snatch it, rush it over to my house on Kenyon Avenue, like a severed limb to be reattached, with the team of musical microsurgeons, the Ascots, assembled to perform the delicate operation and join it to our repertoire. This may not sound like much to you, but believe me, it was an impressive and bold move. The song wasn't even on the radio yet, nobody had heard it, and we were going to perform it live on TV. A coup. We could have even claimed it was a song we "made". After deciphering the code of Mick Jagger's mumbling, we tackled the weird eastern neo-Hindu music, ran through it a few times, hopped in our VW van, and dashed up to Newark for the broadcast.[39]

Disc-O-Teen was a central stop on the thriving New Jersey garage band scene, with (mostly) teenage bands playing schools and clubs throughout the state, including Dodds in Orange, Mothers in Greenwood Lake, D'Jais in Belmar, and the Hullabaloo nightclub in Manville.[40] One rocker remembered, "There were a lot of different types of gigs in those days for underaged bands. We played CYO dances, temple dances, jr. high and high schools and YMCAs. There were even teen clubs like Club 65 in Elizabeth, New Jersey where all the kids went. The Moose and Elks held teen dances as well."[41]

Every year *Disc-O-Teen* held a series of Battles of the Bands, culminating in an annual winner to be awarded a contract with Buddah Records, won in 1965 by Herald Square and 1966 by the Ascots, who later changed their name to the Doughboys and scored a hit single with "Rhoda Mendelbaum."[42] A few, like the Critters, recording on the Kama Sutra label (with the Lovin' Spoonful), reached a level of success, with "Younger Girl" and even charting in the Top 40 with "Mister Dieingly Sad" and "Don't Let the Rain Fall Down On Me." Up-and-coming touring bands, or even nationally known acts such as the Blues Magoos, the Blues Project (with future members of Blood, Sweat and Tears), the Lovin' Spoonful, the Rascals, and the Easybeats visited the show, some even playing or lip-synching, but most judging dance contests and clowning around during the themed episodes. Saturday shows—the only ones not broadcast live—were devoted to themes (including Beach, Hillbilly, Vampire's Ball, Roman, Spy, Dinosaur Egg Roll) so that the regulars would bring a change of costume for the taping on Friday night after the live show.[43]

Touring bands often played Symphony Hall downstairs from Studio A, and *Disc-O-Teen* regulars attended the shows, sometimes even dancing on stage. The Beach Boys visited twice, and regulars spotted them eating at Nick's. When the Rolling Stones played on November 7, 1965, the four finalists from the *Disc-O-Teen* Battle of the Bands opened up, with DOT regulars, dressed in "flapper-fringed 'go-go' outfits," dancing between acts.[44]

The most famous episode featured a visit from the Doors in June 1967. Fresh off the release of their single "Light My Fire," while the song was still rising on the Billboard charts, the Doors signed a rare "trade for mention," which meant they would lip-synch along with the prerecorded song—something that cost the show a great deal more than a mere appearance.[45] Although the band's notoriety was in the future, the kids who followed music knew about the band. Among the regulars, the show has achieved mythic status, clouded in mixed and conflicting memories, with various bands claiming to have appeared as well. The cameraman Joe LoRe' even remembers that the band arrived fresh from the recording studio with a brand new "acetate master" of their unreleased song—but "Light My Fire" had been recorded the previous summer, the album released in January, and the single in May as the second single from the album.[46] One thing *everyone* agrees on, however: "Jim Morrison was a perfect ass, making himself obnoxious on and off camera."[47] Before the show, some of the regulars hung out in Zach's office with members of the band—the keyboardist Ray Manzarek playing with Zach's apple corer and Jim discussing a less-well-known California group called the Godz with one of the regulars.[48] While lip-synching, Morrison fondled the microphone suggestively while leering at the camera.[49]

When Zach interviewed him, Morrison refused to speak, staring blankly ahead and mugging for the camera. Morrison seemed stoned, something that the young dancers of DOT were not (yet) acquainted with. Just before the end of the show, after wandering through the dancers on this Beach Bum–themed episode, Jim turned to Zach and muttered, "This is the freakiest show I've ever seen."[50]

The show faced its greatest challenge during the deadly riots in Newark in July 1967. During the actual week of the riots in July, the shows went on the air with very few dancers. One regular remembers, "I was on that show with only a handful of people. I took the city bus down as usual to Broad Street and I guess many of the other kids parents were smarter about not driving them or not allowing them into the city. The bus stopped running by the time DOT was over and I had no way home so Zak drove me to a friend's house, close to downtown."[51] Richard Scrivani recalls, "Of course nobody was there, three kids came and their father brought them. . . . The Sweet Inspirations also showed up, they lived in Newark. So we had to do the whole show with them singing, and I don't know whether they sang a lot or what happened, it was all lip-synching."[52] Another regular's memory is more typical,

"My sister and I really wanted to go but our parents made us wait a couple of weeks before they felt it was safe enough for us to return."[53]

After the riots, only gradually did parents begin to allow their kids to return to the set: "I wouldn't be attending any shows for some time that summer. In fact I remember watching and seeing hardly any people dancing during that time."[54] The riots highlighted the changing nature of Newark, especially racially. As early as 1966, it was clear that the show would not be immune to outside issues. Richard Scrivani writes,

> As the summer [of 1966] rolled on, more young people from the Newark area got wind of the fact that there was a dancing show being broadcast in their backyard, and since the city had a sizable minority population, the show began reflecting a distinct ethnic diversity. Soon black and Hispanic kids began to outnumber the Caucasian population in the studio (Newark was also comprised of a generous helping of Polish and Italian families), temperaments clashed and tension began to grow. I remember a distinct effort being made to keep the show "balanced," by including a proportionate number of different races, but trouble was looming in spite of it. Fights would sometimes break out outside the Mosque Theater, and there were more than a few times when Keith and I would make tracks across the street to the car to avoid impending trouble.[55]

The scene was fracturing, as the shared identity of the teens was challenged by new arrivals and changing times. The producers of the show did their part to accommodate the new developments, as one regular remembered: "I remember once, asking Barry if I can dance with a black girl (she was always so much fun- but I can't remember her name)? Not only did he say yes, but he put us up on the 'platform' (in the corner, with the 2 posts with the 'cobwebs' connecting them)!!!!! Pretty daring stuff, for 1967!!!!"[56] The show had kept the real world at bay, but only by ignoring it and providing a safe space for kids to create their own world. But it could only last for so long.

The summer of 1967 was the final one for *Disc-O-Teen*. The Beatles released *Sgt. Pepper's Lonely Hearts Club Band* and rock 'n' roll was transformed instantly from something to dance to into something to think about. And smoke pot to.[57] Many of the regulars began to fade away as a new wave of younger teens arrived. Some of those regulars graduated to the New York scene, frequenting the Fillmore East and other rock clubs (where they were sometimes recognized by DOT fans[58]). Scrivani remembers that by last few months of show,

> The usual familiar faces of the "regulars" were for the most part gone also; everyone was getting older, priorities were being shuffled and younger kids started to filter in. In many cases, the kids were so young that *Disc-o-teen* was in danger of resembling a children's show. Even the dancing was changed—the classic sixties dances the original kids had been doing (the "Frug," the "Swim," the "Pony," the "Jerk," etc) was [sic] now replaced by a single gyration which consisted of nothing more than standing in place, knees bending slightly, while moving the arms up and down in time with the music. It wasn't so much dancing as swaying to the beat, and it took so little effort that it just looked silly. Even Zach seemed less interested in the show, his between-the-songs business having lost some of its pizzazz, his talks with the new kids more perfunctory than inspired. The end was near, you could feel it in the air.[59]

The end came suddenly and with little fanfare. The final show, billed as "the two and a half year anniversary" show, was taped on October 31, and broadcast November 4, 1967.[60] Rumors had circulated in the weeks before, so some of the regulars returned. Sue drew a picture of a haunted mansion called "Zaks Place," which she presented to Zacherley.[61] The band Every Mother's Son and a strange character named Brute Force appeared, and Linda P. sang a lip-synch duet of "I Got You, Babe" with Zach.[62] Scrivani remembers:

> The show ended with Zach climbing onto the bandstand, gently shooing off the array of newcomers dancing there, replacing them with the small group of original regulars, all dancing to the Dave Clark Five's version of "You Got What It Takes." Joe's camera dollied back, far into the nether regions of the vast studio, the tiny figures swaying to the music seeming to wave "goodbye" for the last time, John Zacherle doing his famous "underarm" dance on center stage. Fadeout. No one watching the show outside of the inner circle had a clue that it would not be on the next day or any other day. *Disc-o-teen* was gone with a whimper.[63]

Mark, who was a regular on the last season, recalls being quite aware of the ending: "If my memory serves me right, at the end of the very last show, the camera pulled all the way to the back of the studio showing a distant shot of the whole set. Me, being VERY MUCH AWARE that the show (and DOT itself) was ending, I decided to wave good-bye (I believe I'm towards the left side of the screen - there were [sic] no one in front of me and my partner). The reason I know all this, is because I watched the last show that Saturday and cried that this was the end."[64]

The producer Barry Landers remembers the sadness at the end:

When Eddie Cooperstein and Herb Greene decided that they were going to kill the show, I mean, that was like death. It was like somebody died. It was like a stake literally through our hearts, honest to goodness. Zach wanted to make sure it was low-key. A very quiet day, very somber day. The girls were crying, we all were. It was like a big dark cloud descended upon the entire place, and we didn't want to talk about it. We didn't discuss it in the control room, we didn't discuss it in the office. Zach was trying to be as stiff-upper-lipped as he possibly could, but I know he was heartbroken. . . . Everybody was.[65]

After the taping, the regulars gathered around Zach's car, decorating it with art and messages.[66] Zach collected the self-addressed envelopes from the regulars, in which he later sent them individual, handwritten notes thanking them "for making DOT such a fun show to watch."[67] Landers describes the dynamics of DOT, "The kids made the show. And Zach just had this great love for them, you know, and they loved him, they just *adored* him. And the crew did too."[68] Zacherley was unfailingly "charming and polite."[69] The personal touch from Zach was something felt by all who encountered him. Kids came to the show starstruck, in awe to meet the great television star Zacherley, a "magnetic" and mesmerizing performer to a young teenager.[70] And they all came away with a real personal connection to a charismatic yet humble gentleman, one who kept in touch with many of the regulars until his death, fifty years later, in 2016 at the age of ninety-eight.

5 • THE UPSTAGE CLUB AND THE ASBURY PARK SCENE

No man towers over New Jersey music history more than Bruce Springsteen. And the rock world he emerged from in Asbury Park has its place firmly established in rock history. The world he inhabited at the Stone Pony is the stuff of legend. But less is known about the scene that preceded the "Glory Days."

If *Disc-O-Teen* and the garage band explosion emerged on the heels of Beatlemania in the mid-1960s, by the end of the decade, after the Summer of Love and Woodstock, rock was an established institution in American culture—and the methods of plugging into that global network occurred on the local level. In Asbury Park the local kids and musicians bridged the world of the 1960s and 1970s at the Upstage Club. Asbury Park had long had a reputation for summer fun with a honky-tonk flavor. The boardwalk, amusement parks, and beach beckoned day-trippers to the Jersey Shore. By the 1960s, the town had a well-worn edge, with a bit of an anything-goes feel to it—a place to slough off the week's toil and let loose.

What we know as "The Sixties" was made on the ground level, in daily life, not just in the mass media. For young people letting loose in the 1960s, Asbury was the place to go to play out of the prying eyes of parents. Young people cruised the Circuit, a mile-long loop that bordered the coastline and circled back, the avenues dotted with clubs, bars, and hangouts, racing in the streets, chasing members of the opposite sex, tossing fireworks, hitchhiking, greasers taunting the longhairs, and doing their best to avoid the law for the crimes of sleeping on the beach or loitering or going barefoot on the boardwalk.[1] Asbury was just a bit weirder than the average Jersey Shore town.

In the 1960s, there were all sorts of places to fool around in Asbury, and lots of bars and clubs, so there was a critical mass of local and nearby musicians playing the Circuit, as well as youngsters inspired by the folk scene in Greenwich Village, Beatlemania, and the hardening sounds of rock in the Summer of Love in places like San Francisco, Los Angeles, New York, and London. Asbury had a multitude of places to play. Visiting major acts could play the Convention Hall and the Paramount Theatre. "The local music scene," Steven Van Zandt claims, "was unlike any local scene before our time or after. For the only time in history there were dozens of places for teenagers to hang out and see live rock bands. High school dances, VFW halls, union halls, all the beach clubs in Sea Bright, coffee houses, colleges, festivals in parks, and even a night club called the 'Teendezvous.' There were also a lot of music shows on T.V."[2] Other clubs like the Hullabaloo (later the Sunshine In) and the Student Prince, only wanted Top-40 cover bands. So, musicians would work those paying gigs, where they played what the owners wanted and fans danced to, but they had no place to explore and create their own music. It was only at the Upstage Club that a new sort of scene could develop.

The Upstage Club arose from the unlikely pairing of a married couple of hairdressers. Tom Potter was a singular character—a "wacky, big, burly, bearded, larger-than-life, profane man."[3] Injured while training as a paratrooper during World War II and honorably discharged at the rank of corporal, Tom attended the beauty school at Wilfred Academy in Newark and went to work in the family beauty salon after the war. But at various times he also owned a "Fix-It-Shop" and a cruise-chartering business, took classes in photography and art, produced works of fiction, paintings, sculptures, photomontages, and judged beauty contests—all while finding the time for a couple of marriages. In 1961, Tom met nineteen-year-old Margaret, twenty years his junior, who became the third Mrs. Potter. Tom's unpredictable, artistic spirit was a perfect match for Margaret's adventurous, competitive nature.[4]

Together they owned a beauty shop on the second floor of a Cookman Avenue walkup up in Asbury Park, with their apartment on the third floor and a roof garden. A "surreal place, complete with Tom's abstract drawings and sculptures . . . the Potter house became a gathering place for musicians, artists, photographers, and poets," according to Tom's granddaughter and biographer Carrie Potter-Devening. "On weekends you could expect the unexpected."[5] The environment was "like Beatniks meet Hippies."[6]

There, Margaret learned guitar and formed her band Margaret and the Distractions. Tom became allergic to the dyes and chemicals involved in hairdressing and photography, and looked around for other ways to foster his artistic drive and make a living. And the parties kept getting bigger, outgrowing the confines of their apartment.

Margaret Potter remembered the all-night sessions when she would invite musicians over after their gigs:

So that's how it started, that way. I'd have a couple people over and one evening I conned them into trading guitar lessons for breakfast. Alright? So, as I gradually learned to play the guitar, and these people came over, it began to grow. The next thing you knew, as I learned to play and as other people heard about it, you know I'd just throw an extra pot of coffee on, the next thing you knew, like maybe two or three bands in the local area were coming over for breakfast, and were bringing their instruments, alright . . . sitting there and waiting till there was a free instrument. I mean, they would play all night, then sit and play till daylight. So, my husband, who was a hairdresser, became allergic to hair dye, so he couldn't do hair anymore, and he says, you know, there has to be a way—these musicians, you know, they don't ever want to stop playing— there has to be a way to make a living out of it and for them to have a place . . . to go and do this.[7]

Tom began to think of a coffeehouse or club, "partly to get all of those people out of his house, but also as a means of filling a need in the community. He became keen to provide a place where the musicians could sit and play for hours and do whatever they wanted."[8]

With a partner, Tom conceived the Upstage Club as an indoor extension of the Circuit, and Margaret quickly became "the driving force behind the club that began from a spark of Tom's imagination."[9] Tom came from an older generation, but he recognized the wild youth in his midst, especially as the hippie counterculture emerged in full bloom by 1967. Hippie youth lived in local boardinghouses, crashed on each other's floors, or rented cheap walkups. Younger kids flocked to Asbury for the freedom of its boardwalk. And the lingua franca of youth was rock music.

Tom rented a space two doors down from his apartment "to create a place where musicians could come and play and hang with each other."[10] Potter had a specific vision that would nurture the musical environment, allowing musicians not only to perform, but to play with each other, to jam and hang out, exchanging ideas and sounds. Joe Petillo, sixteen years old and hanging out at the all-night apartment sessions while playing in Margaret's band, remembers Tom seeking his counsel—after he had already rented the space: "Whenever Tom had an idea, it was hard not to get caught up in his enthusiasm. I can still remember walking up the stairs for the first time and hearing him describe what the place would be like. And sure enough, 50 gallons of black paint, a few dozen mannequins painted day glow, several dozen backlights later, we were open for business."[11]

The venue began as a 1960s coffeehouse on the second floor, above a Thom McAn shoe store, the space painted by the local kids in Day-Glo colors and festooned with fishnetting and a large, fluorescent green mermaid that gave the space its name. As a regular patron Albee Tellone remembered, "It was an incubator of musical creativity. . . . It was a place that allowed for the creative juices of young musicians to flow freely."[12] The club was envisioned as part of the larger counterculture, with showings of avant-garde films and art. "The weird thing about it, and the cool thing about it, was that it was a place to get things organized," remembered one regular. "Like any kind of activist type of event. People would come from all over the place to Upstage and bring flyers, so you knew what was going on in New Brunswick. Back then, New Brunswick was the other music spot in New Jersey. And it was strange, you'd have Black Panthers coming over there and dropping stuff off. You know what's going on with them and things. Organizations that were anti-establishment and stuff."[13]

Soon, the Potters' vision expanded to the third floor, where they created a large open room for loud rock music and began the jam sessions for which the venue is still remembered. In March 1968, the *Asbury Park Press* reported on the opening of the Upstage Club as "a new discotheque-coffeehouse-nightclub here, for young people too old for teen-age clubs and too young for bars." Potter told the *Press*, "I feel it's time to treat them as grownups. . . . But there'll be no booze and no pot!" Annual dues for club membership was $12. The *Press* described the decor as "pop art collages and psychedelic designs painted on black walls with paint that glows under the ultra-violet lights." And the article concluded by reiterating that Tom Potter would not tolerate any drug use: "At the top of the stairs is a glowing poster in which Smokey the Bear warns, 'All grass fires will be put out of this joint!' Mr. Potter is adamant in his aversion to marijuana. 'I don't feel it's necessary to get turned on,' he says."[14] Although there is no evidence that people smoked pot inside the Upstage Club, there is also no reason to believe that Tom Potter's perspective persuaded anyone to abstain from the countercultural drug of choice.

"Tom and Margaret Potter had a different vision and it was multi-layered," according to Albee Tellone. "No drugs or drinking were tolerated and Tom ruled with an iron fist. . . . They wanted the young people to have a place to go and dance but also a place for musicians to stretch their imagination. . . . They had a choice whether to hang out with the 'Folkies' in the Mermaid or go upstairs to dance or listen to an all night jam. It was the only public eatery with music that was open until 5am."[15] Tom and Margaret created a space where young people could hang out, and they fed many an urchin for free in the wee hours. Margaret's spaghetti seems to have kept a whole generation alive. "There was no place anywhere like the Upstage," remembered David Mieras, a club regular. "That place was totally in a league of its own. It was very, very different. It was a really avant-garde place, very art-oriented, individualized and where people found an identity. It was like your club. There was no liquor there, but you'd identify it as your club. Most people had passes to get in. . . . We could care less about getting into a bar because we had the Upstage. It was the greatest place. I mean, we just had so much fun there it was incredible."[16]

An Upstage regular, Robbin Thompson, remembers the space as a product of the times. "Every city and town in the 60's and early 70's had a place that was, in its own way, like The Upstage," claims Thompson. "It was a gathering place for the musicians of the community, a place where the 'hip' could go and not get hassled for their left of center views or the length of their hair. It was also a place where those who pretended to be normal humans workin' a regular 9 to 5 could go and be what they really wanted to be." It took someone older to recognize the need and to bring the vision to life. "It was always run by a person that was a little bit older than us, a little bit hipper than us. Someone who knew that when they were younger there was a need for a place where we could get away, feel like we were amongst friends that understood. A place where there was a non-parental ear ready to listen and give advice."[17] Tom and Margaret created a type of space that was rarely found outside major cities, and in that space arose a unique scene. The counterculture was bursting into the national consciousness as a phenomenon, but hippies still felt—and were treated—like outsiders. For the hippies, the Upstage became a refuge from harassment by the "greasers" or the cops. "Remember," Robbin Thompson notes, "there weren't a lot of places you could get into with long hair, and we all had long hair."[18]

At 11:00 P.M. the youngsters under eighteen would be kicked out of the third floor because of local curfew laws (though they would occasionally sneak back in behind the backs of the bouncers black Tiny and white Tiny), retreating to the protective space of the Green Mermaid under Tom and Margaret's watchful eyes. The third-floor space would shut down for an hour from Midnight to 1:00 A.M., and reopen with live music. During the hour, musicians would go out for air, visit a bar, and, no doubt, despite Tom's stern decree, smoke some pot or indulge in whatever other drugs were available. Returning at 1:00 A.M., and joining with the other musicians who were filing in after their own gigs, the musicians would be assigned a spot by Tom.

Tom was the acknowledged patriarch, adored, respected, and even feared, but now over forty, abrasive, and of a different mindset from that of the young people. It was Tom who encouraged every new idea with a "'Sure do it.' . . . He would make you seize the initiative to make it happen, he would give you the environment, and he would give you the support and you had to come through and do it."[19]

But it was Margaret, the "gravel throated, chain smoking tough cookie guitar player," who became the creative force behind the evolving environment.[20] With her as the charismatic leader, Margaret and the Distractions acted as house band, while also playing the whole Jersey Shore scene. "It was Margaret who encouraged 'open jamming' when the scheduled bands were on break and usually the entire last hour or so from 4am to 5am was reserved for jamming," remembers Albee Tellone. "It was Margaret who made us feel at home there. She was the reason we came back night after night and braved the bellowing of a tipsy Tom. She was the helmsman at the wheel of a turbulent ship. For the guys and gals that worked there, she was like a big sister or even a sort of den mother. She made sure we were happy there. Lots of times she invited us over to her apartment for spaghetti and meatballs."[21] Tom, too, is credited with feeding many a starving kid or musician at the Green Mermaid, but Tellone recalls, "You never knew if he was going to hug you or kick your ass out the door. . . . Margaret always watched over us younger musicians."[22]

And Tom ran the show, assigning time slots and assembling the jams. Vini "Mad Dog" Lopez claims, "Tom's the one that co-ordinated the whole thing. You would come here with your band and gotta go to Tom and see if you could play. He'd say, 'What do you play?' 'I play bass.' 'Ok, go over there and talk to Vinny for a minute 'cos you're playing with him.' He wouldn't let the bands play together."[23] Sometimes full bands would play, but often, and especially as the night wore on, jams would evolve, with players slotting in and out without the jam even stopping. The folklorist Susan Etta Keller notes that the Upstage offered an opportunity "for the type of informal musical interaction that was not available elsewhere. It was jamming that provided the special, largely nonverbal connection that set the community apart. Jamming was less structured than the song-oriented music normally played. . . . It also allowed musicians to play with people outside of their band, and for those without bands to have an opportunity to play. . . . The jamming provided new, less formal, and perhaps more comfortable sources of community for these individual musicians."[24]

The most distinctive feature of the Upstage was the wall of speakers. The musician John Mulrenan described how Tom put the sound system together:

There was a hallway behind the stage that went into Tom Potter's office and the back of the stage was a plywood wall he had erected. He had a bunch of used guitar ampheads that he'd buy from kids. They'd tell him, "I gotta sell my amp." He'd say, "Ok, I'll give you 70 bucks kid." So he had about five of the old Fender guitar heads up there. And then people would bring him a speaker, like an old car radio speaker or whatever they wanted to sell to make a couple of bucks. He would take a saw and just saw a hole in the plywood, take wood screws, screw the speaker to the wall and then just jump it over to the other speakers with two wires. So you had this wall in back, it was all random speakers wired up to these ampheads with no rhyme or reason. And everybody would just come up and plug into the amps and play. The amps were hooked up to the back speakers with just wood screwed into the back wall. There was pieces of plywood just hanging there. It was speakers not being enclosed in an actual enclosure. All of these different weirdo speakers, half of them blown and stuff.[25]

Billy Ryan helped put the system together, selling Tom his two 58 Fender Basement Tweed amplifiers—"They were and are still the finest guitar amplifiers that money can buy"—that Tom took out of the original boxes put them in the wall.

> There were 4 outputs in each of the Fender Basements. Now you had 8 outputs and 8 guitar players could play at once! And for the speakers he has got the 10's there. So he's got eight 10's which a normal amplifier had and then he took all those 8 inch for mid range and he wired it all up to these two 50 watt two Fender basement amplifiers. So he had a 100 watts running all of those speakers. He might have had a PA plugged into the other speakers so that whole thing was a wall of guitar sound and the public address system all at once.[26]

"The sound was just God awful good," according to Big Danny Gallagher.[27] "What made the Upstage different than the rest was the fact that from a musician standpoint it was set up for anyone to walk in and play with the greatest of ease because the amps and speakers were already there, set up and built into the wall of the stage," remembers Robbin Thompson. "It was an awesome thing. Any musician could walk in with their guitar or whatever and just plug in to the floor or the wall and rock! . . . It was like a rock n roll testing area."[28]

A coterie of regulars developed, supplemented by a stream of newcomers, youngsters, amateurs, and rank amateurs. Blues provided the framework, a simple formula for all to riff off of, and the basis for much of the guitar-based rock that dominated the era. Margaret Potter understood the dynamics of how the music provided a way to create a scene: "Blues is a very feeling kind of music . . . you're given three different guitar players, same blues progression and you're going to get something different. Alright, put five up there and you're going to get five different interpretations and they'll all be right, because it's—it leaves so much room for freedom." And blues rock is as simple a musical formula as there is, allowing both the beginner to enter the jam and the virtuoso to explore, create, and express. Thus, the music itself became the foundation for the scene. As Keller concludes, "Ideally, this mirrored, and perhaps helped constitute, the attitude of community as a whole toward its members."[29]

Although Tom was nominally in charge, it appears, in retrospect and memory, that Margaret steered the situation, and she was dedicated to creating a "spirit of inclusiveness" and tolerance: "I think that, that's a camaraderie, that in other words, you weren't trying to fight musicians; you had musicians tuned in, trying to make you better. . . . And that forms unbreakable ties."[30] As Tom envisioned, hanging around, whether in his back office drinking beers from his "beererator" or in the Green Mermaid eating sandwiches or up on the third floor, on- or offstage, became the foundation for a scene devoted to music and a way of life. Jamming onstage cemented those bonds, as Margaret discovered continually,

> I can't begin to tell you the things that happened. On stage. Instantly. Boom, and you're like, "Oh my gosh, listen to this!" You know, it would come out of nowhere. . . . They couldn't believe that it happened, something happened that was so tight and so together, in an instant. And, you walk off stage, and, and you surprise yourself, let's put it that way. You surprise yourself, you know, you say, "Oh wow." You know, you'd be playing it, and you'd look at the other guy on the stage and see the smile on his face and you knew, see, you know what I'm saying? You knew, and you'd say, "Whoa, listen to this," and you were doing it, but you were still saying listen to this [laughs]. It's quite a feeling.[31]

This is not to say that the scene was fully democratic. There was clearly, as Sonny Kenn, already Asbury's most accomplished musician, discovered, a "pecking order . . . and if everybody saw you could play, it was cool."[32] To those who were just honing their chops, the scene could be intimidating. "I remember going to the Upstage, but I was not good enough, I would say, to be quite frank, to get up on stage with those guys and play," according to one regular, Robert Santelli. "The competition at the Upstage was so keen, so intense, that you really had to be a good player."[33] Another teen remembered, "Sneaking out my bedroom window on a regular basis, I would meet up with kids from Bradley, or Deal, either at the pavilion, or at the Boardwalk or along the way and go to the Upstage. Getting on stage was not always easy in the beginning, for there was certainly a pecking order starting with the regular players and working its way to the new guys."[34]

Generally, however, there was a mixture on stage, as Tom Potter orchestrated things to foster the musical interchange. Often, musicians had to earn their place, demonstrating their improvement over time, so that eventually they would be invited into the later jams with the better musicians. It depended, also, on what instrument you played. Guitarists were a dime a dozen, so there was keen competition. Drummers, however, were at a premium, so Bobby Williams and Vini Lopez played with all the better musicians. Keller notes that a "relatively small circle of people" came to form the core of the better jams: "Members of the group were not necessarily snobbish, but amidst all the openness of the establishment, they did find a relatively small circle of people with whom they felt the most comfortable."[35]

The inclusiveness really built around the dedication, even more than skill. Those who showed up nightly, who threw themselves into the scene, who devoted themselves to the music and the lifestyle, became the core. The club itself demanded as much, since things did not really start rocking until after 1:00 A.M. "We would finish our gigs and stroll up here with our axes and play great music," according to Gerry Carboy. "What more can you say? That's what this place was about—camaraderie."[36] Santelli recalls, "If you were too young or you had to work the next day . . . staying up to 4 or 5 in the morning was a difficult thing to do, so you really had to be dedicated to go to the Upstage."[37] And those musicians who did so were generally the ones whose playing continued to improve. "That's where I learned," Kevin Kavanaugh remembers. "It's one thing to learn how to play on your own. It is another thing entirely to play with other guys and develop the chemistry it takes to work together. That's how you perfect your craft, listening to and working together with other musicians."[38]

They would all make up the audience for each other, so that there was a kind of equality between performer and viewer that was absent in regular clubs. "When you're working a lot, you never really get to interface with anybody else other than the guys you're playing with on the gigs," recalls Carboy. "You go up there and you see guys you haven't seen in months and say 'Hey, how you doing? You're off today . . . . Yeah!' At 3 o'clock there would be guys that just finished gigs on the boardwalk and they'd be strolling in with their axes and stuff." It was "a great scene for musicians meeting musicians."[39] And at 5:00 A.M. they would clean up, maybe walk over to the pier and go fishing at dawn.

Indeed, most of the regulars were not just there as musicians but as members of the club and full participants in the scene. They are the ones who helped Tom realize his artistic vision by painting the Day-Glo designs on the walls and building the stage. "Some of them spent every night, every weekend the club was open, and they worked and they played together, and I mean for nothing, food, and for the love of music."[40] As they used to joke, the Upstage was the cheapest hotel in town, as you could stay there all night and then spend the day sleeping on the beach. "I got a job working the door there and my whole life changed," claims Big Danny Gallagher. "I mean, rock and roll as a lifestyle had never come in front of me before. I saw it and said, 'Well, this is it!'"[41] Southside Johnny came to the jams religiously:

> I lived a half-mile away so I would go over there just about every night. Some-times I'd go over right from work if I worked late at the post office, which I did for ten months, and I'd still have my post office stuff on. We used to do eight shows a night, eight sets a night, 40–45 minutes each. We were making songs up because we ran out of material. I mean, no matter how many songs you knew you'd do a week's worth of eight shows a night. And you don't want to repeat yourself, do the same songs over and over again-screw that! So we would make stuff up.[42]

In a history of popular music scenes in New Jersey, Asbury deserves a key place, of that there is no doubt. And the Upstage Club earned its spot, even if it had not produced any famous names. But we cannot talk about this story—and possibly not many would be all that interested in this story—without Springsteen ("The Boss"). Through all the layers of hagiography and nostalgia, one thing shines through: from the moment Bruce Springs-teen arrived in Asbury Park, it was clear to all that this man was something special. Just about every account carries the same tone . . . Who is this guy?

Springsteen had been playing in Jersey bands for a while, so some people already knew of him, but he arrived, looking gaunt and raggedy in his torn jeans with a rope belt, sometime in the wee hours of February 23, 1969, and immediately made an impression. "Is it okay if I play my guitar here tonight?" Bruce asked. "Go ahead and plug in," Margaret Potter replied.[43] Springsteen had visited the Upstage a week or so previously to scope out the Downtown Tangiers Band and immediately figured, "This is the coolest place I've ever seen in my life."[44] He also knew that this was a place he could display his tal-ents. So, he plugged his new goldtop Les Paul into an amp and turned it up: "I came to stun."[45] And stun he did—instantly. "That quickly, he took over the room," Tom's son Geoff Potter remembers. "And within five minutes, you couldn't hear a sound except for his guitar," as all eyes and ears turned to the stage.[46] Springsteen, with no need for false modesty, writes in his autobiog-raphy, "I plugged into Tom's mighty wall, stood back and kicked into 'Rock Me Baby,' cutting loose with everything I had. I fried the paint off the place with all the guitar pyrotechnics and wizardry my eighteen-year-old fingers could muster. . . . I watched people sit up, move closer and begin to pay serious attention."[47]

Margaret ran down to the second floor looking for the local guitar legend Sonny Kenn, telling him, "You've gotta get up here!" Watching Springsteen jam with the locals Big Bad Bobby Williams on drums and Vinnie Roslin on bass, Kenn thought, "'Oh my God, he's got it!' Somehow that skinny kid was larger than life!"[48] Another regular concurred: "You couldn't take your eyes off of him. Bruce had this presence. The hairs on the back of your neck would tingle. He had an instinct, a gift."[49]

As the playing continued, Vini Lopez—who had already been talking about Bruce—took over on drums and Danny Federici joined on keyboard, for another forty-five-minute jam. According to the Springsteen biographer Peter Carlin, "The crowd members who weren't pasted against the stage were dancing and spinning across the floor. When Bruce sweated through his T-shirt, he peeled it off and tossed it, *splat*, into the corner of the stage."[50] Springsteen writes, "The insane wall of speakers was vibrating so hard I thought the whole place might just cave onto the shoe-store sales floor below. It all held for thirty something scorching minutes of guitar Armageddon, then I walked off."[51]

After the jam, basking in the afterglow downstairs in the Green Mermaid, Vini Lopez blurted out what he had been thinking of since seeing Bruce play the week before: "Oh geez, let's make a band."[52] On that night Child was born. Later renamed Steel Mill, the band was Springsteen's first including Upstage regulars. Over the coming years he would form the Bruce Springsteen Band and, finally, the E Street Band including musicians he had met and jammed with at the Upstage.

Margaret Potter, like most everyone else, vividly recalls that first encounter with Springsteen, though some of the details differ in her various tellings of the story:

I certainly do remember when Bruce came in for the first time and when I heard him play guitar. That I'll never forget. We were all on stage playing and we took a break. This young man came up to me and said, "The man downstairs said you wouldn't mind if I played your guitar." I said, "Oh sure no problem." He said, "Well, would you show me the system, you know, how it works?" and I said, "Sure!" I brought him up on the stage and just explained how the system was set up. To the right of the stage was a booth so I went and sat down on the booth just to listen and see if he got the idea of the system.

Well, in very little time, I knew he was gonna have no problem. It was amazing. The only thing I can tell you is that the hairs on the back of my neck stood up. He played 15 notes and I thought, "Whew! Let me go downstairs and get some people to see this boy!" and that's what I did. I went downstairs and I don't remember exactly who was in the back room, I know my husband was there. I'm pretty sure that Steven Van Zandt was there, Vini Lopez was there maybe John Luraschi, but I'm not sure. And I said, "Look guys, I think you better get upstairs because this . . . I just have a feeling that he is gonna be great. . . ."

There were a lot of guitar players around and when he came back and played you knew it was pretty obvious, and we were waiting, looking to see what the reactions of the people were. Of course they were musicians there and they were just like, "Where did this guy come from?" and that was kind of the general feeling.[53]

Perhaps the cult of Bruce is so strong that there is a Jersey-wide code of omerta, or maybe some Stalinist historical revisionism, but it is impossible to find one eyewitness to Bruce's arrival at the Upstage who was anything less than stunned. Southside Johnny said:

One night, I walked up and there's this long-haired guy with a gold Les Paul. He's telling this long involved story about going to Catholic school and how they mistreated him and all that stuff. But one day they had music appreciation and Sister Mary brought in a B. B. King album and the hook was that the nuns at Saint Catherine taught me the blues or something like that. He was just so charismatic and funny and good, playing great guitar and his lyrics were coming out and they were these tons of phrases. I thought who the fuck is this guy? Immediately I felt territorial! But it was like wow, he's really good.[54]

Guitars dominated the rock scene at the time, and the most intense competition among musicians in the age of Hendrix, Clapton, Townshend, and Page, was among the lead guitar players. "You'd go to Upstage and there was like three keyboard players," according to Tony Amato. "You had David Sancious, Danny Federici, and Kevin Kavanaugh, the original keyboardist from the Jukes. That was the keyboard players. Drummers you've got Bobby Williams, Vini Lopez, you had about fifteen drummers. You know, a thousand guitar players, five hundred bass players. Because at the time Led Zeppelin was big, Hendrix was big and power trios."[55]

Although Bruce would go on to fame as a songwriter and front man, he was originally recognized for his work on guitar. "Tom Potter introduced me to Bruce up at the Upstage," remembers John Mulrenan. "The first time I sort of noticed him was when Southside Johnny was downstairs playing an out of tune 12-string guitar. So, I'm watching Johnny play this song, but I'm hearing great guitar licks coming out—lead guitar, beautiful melodies. I'm like what the hell is that? So, I walk around the back and Bruce is sitting on the steps, in back of the stage so nobody can see him, playing a Les Paul guitar. I was like wow! This guy can really play."[56] Billy Ryan similarly recalls the moment he was sitting in the club and Carl "Tinker" West said to him, "'Wait 'til you hear this guy I just discovered him!' I'm thinking 'what could he be?' And he plays and he's doing these things, which I'd heard of guitar players doing and I was just blown away."[57]

And Bruce's legendary charisma and star power were immediately apparent. "One time I saw him at the Upstage and he just blew the crowd away," Mulrenan continued.

> He had real long hair, half-way down his chest and no shirt on. His hair was in front of his face so you couldn't even see his face and he looked like he weighed about 80 pounds or so. I was in the audience watching him. He was doing mostly Allman Brothers songs. And then I saw what looked like heat waves coming off of him like energy. Then I felt the crowd around me reacting to those waves. They were reacting to him in a way I'd never seen anybody react to anybody on stage before. That's when I really started paying attention to him.[58]

Springsteen's presence was felt throughout the scene at the Upstage, even when he was not performing. Among the kids who hung out at the Green Mermaid, Bruce had a mystique. David Mieras from Ocean Grove explained:

> We'd sit over in the corner in the dark like little wise guys. I remember the first night Bruce came in. He must have seen all of us kids from somewhere before because he came in and he had these dark sunglasses on. It was so funny. I'll never forget it. He came up and his hair was real long, he had dark sunglasses on and he had like a fringe jacket, I believe. I looked at him and said wow, who is that? He just came up to the top of the stairs and stood there. It was like who's this guy?[59]

The teenage girls developed a game where they tried to tap the males in the butt with their spoons, calling themselves "Spoon Ladies," and Bruce was their favorite target.[60] At the Green Mermaid, Bruce played with Albee Tellone's Hired Hands in the acoustic jams.[61]

Springsteen himself delivered a tribute to the Upstage in the liner notes to Southside Johnny's debut 1976 album *I Don't Want to Go Home*. Recognizing the value of the community of musicians, Springsteen noted, "There were a lotta musicians there 'cause the bands that came down from North Jersey and New York to play in the Top 40 clubs along the shore would usually end up their regular gig, along . . . with a lotta different guys from the local areas. Everybody went there 'cause it was open later than the regular clubs and because between 1 and 5 in the morning you could play pretty much whatever you wanted, and if you were good enough, you could choose the guys you wanted to play with."[62] And if you weren't all that good you could still jump into the jams. It wasn't only about skill, but about community and rock and roll as a way of life:

There were these guys . . . Mad Dog Lopez, Big Danny, Fast Eddie Larachi, his brother Little John, Margaret & The Distractions (house band), Black Tiny, White Tiny, Miami Steve, and assorted E Streeters, plus the heaviest drummer of them all, in terms of both poundage and sheer sonic impact, Biiiiig Baaaaand Bobby Williams, badass king of hearts, so tough he'd go to the limit for you every time, all night. You will never see most of these names on another record besides this one, but nonetheless, they're names that should be spoken in reverence at least once, not 'cause they were great musicians (truth is, some of them couldn't play nothin' at all), but because they were each in their own way living spirit of what, to me, rock'n'roll is all about. It was *music as survival*, and they lived it down their souls, night after night.[63]

Music as survival—a phrase as good as any to capture the spirit of Springsteen's whole career, a spirit that was nurtured at the Upstage.

As Bruce wrote, "Some of them couldn't play nothin' at all," but some others were extremely talented musicians who would go on to build careers making music, and a few would even achieve fame, most notably including Bruce's own E Street Band and Southside Johnny and the Asbury Jukes. Although he had already had a couple of bands before arriving at the Upstage in 1969, it was there that he began to pull the threads together.

Quickly establishing himself as a regular, he was paid $20 a night by Tom to perform, and he jammed regularly with the locals. It was at Upstage that Bruce pulled together a musical revue called "Doctor Zoom and the Sonic Boom" that consisted of many of the regulars, including some of the waitresses and bouncers, performing cover songs amid much spectacle. Asked to open for the Allman Brothers at a local club, Bruce decided, according to Kevin Kavanaugh, "I don't really feel like doing it, let's just everybody come on, we'll all get together and we'll do this then."[64] Bruce regularly jammed from 1969 to the club's closing in October 1971, taking the lead in presenting what were known as Bruce Springsteen Jam Concerts. His band Steel Mill played its farewell shows for the Upstage on January 22 and 23, 1971.[65]

As with *Disc-O-Teen*, the comfortable scene could not survive the turmoil of the era and the real world forever. The beginning of the end for the Upstage came with the Asbury Park riots the week of July 4, 1970. Asbury Park had been segregated since its founding in the nineteenth century. Built by the businessman James A. Bradley in 1871, the town had experienced tension over racial mixing from its inception. As early as 1885, the Asbury Park *Daily Journal* pronounced the town "a white peoples resort" and complained in an editorial that "the colored people are becoming a nuisance." Although the *Journal* acknowledged the rights of African Americans to the vote and the rule of law, "when it comes to social intermingling then we object most strenuously and emphatically." Henceforth, "the colored folk" would be welcome as servants and employees, but not as beachgoers and promenaders along the boardwalk.[66] Controversy flared from time to time, and African American leaders pushed back continually, but by 1970, Asbury Park, like most cities in the United States was riven with inequality and racial discrimination, with blacks relegated to the West Side neighborhoods, away from the beach. African Americans were recruited to Asbury Park as service workers in the resort industry, but segregation and discrimination kept much of the black population in poverty, living in dire rat-infested housing, with poor employment opportunities.[67] White flight had begun in the 1960s—as it had in cities all across the country, fostered by government policies promoting suburbanization, racist bank lending policies, and discriminatory real estate practices—but the process accelerated after the outbreak of violence against property that erupted in 1970.

When on July 4, two teen dances took place and then emptied out into the streets, bottles were thrown, cops were called, crowds formed and dispersed.[68] The riots began at a youth dance at the West Side Community Center and spread across the business district. Over the course of the coming week, violence flared regularly along and around Springfield Avenue. By the end of the week, 180 people had been injured (including 15 police officers), 167 had been arrested, and $4 million of property damage had been tallied. While most of the damage was on the black West Side, the damage to Asbury's reputation was irreversible. Destroyed buildings had still not been replaced decades later. Tourists stopped coming. Locals and neighbors stopped shopping downtown.[69]

The riots of 1970 in Asbury Park nearly destroyed the downtown and shook the music scene. The Upstage had only a tenuous relationship with the black world of Asbury Park and the black musical world. Obviously, the music played at the Upstage was rooted in the African American tradition, and there were musicians who worked both worlds. But the rock world was resegregating musically, and Asbury was no exception. Although Motown and much Top-40 music were still mixed, guitar-based rock was moving away from the dance music that was developing out of R&B and soul—with Southside Johnny a glaring exception. Photos from the Upstage show a degree of racial integration, but the scene was largely separate from what was happening in the black clubs. "I was playing on the other side of the tracks then," remembers J. T. Bowen: "The Orchid Lounge, the Turf Club, all these clubs were on the Black side of town."[70]

The scholar Craig Hansen Werner argues that Springsteen resisted this trend: "At a time when white rock was sounding whiter and black music was sounding blacker . . . , Springsteen refused to surrender the populist energy of sixties rock and soul."[71] Springsteen acknowledged, "There was racial tension" in the rock world and around the Asbury Park scene, "but it was also a place where people mixed. I walked into the Upstage and saw [the black pianist] David Sancious. I met [the black sax player] Clarence [Clemons]. We had one of the first integrated bands in rock music—that was something that grew up around Asbury Park."[72] David Sancious remembers feeling wary, conscious of the very real possible consequences of crossing the racial borderline of Asbury Park. "I was nervous about it," Sancious admits. "It wasn't a place where black people went."[73] Used to playing with R&B bands at the Orchid Lounge, he did feel welcome at the Upstage when he arrived as a fifteen-year-old keyboardist, finding a "sense of community" built around the common love of rock 'n' roll. The Upstage provided an oasis from the outside world where there was "no funky racial vibe at all" among the musicians.[74]

The riots themselves were experienced only slightly by the Upstage crowd. Springsteen watched the West Side burn from atop a water tower on the roof of the surfboard factory he was living in on the outskirts of town.[75] Some vividly remember getting out of the club as the riots began and that the doorman got a shotgun from his car.[76] Tom and some regulars created a barricade on the stairs out of bar chairs, deterring invaders.[77] Jim Fanier recalled, "I was sitting by the first landing of the stairs holding a shotgun listening to the noise outside and the door opened. Someone had a lit liquor bottle, Molotov cocktail, I said 'GO AWAY!' They ran off without shutting the door!"[78] The club was closed for the week, as the town was under curfew at sundown.

Bobby Williams remembers the effect of the riots on the scene at the Upstage: "I remember when the riots hit in 1970, that was sort of the beginning of the end. You could almost—you almost knew the end was coming. . . . Things were never the same after that. They just weren't. Of course, you didn't have people coming down here like they used to."[79] Joe Petillo was stunned by the riots and their aftermath, which he described as "a surprising dagger in the heart of musicians around here because this was an environment where color never mattered."[80] In the sheltered world of the club, the kids could escape the realities of the outside world. After the riots, that was no longer possible, and they were confronted with a reality that they had been able to ignore. Another regular remembers that although "it was all peace and love in the Upstage," the broken windows and burned out buildings along Springfield Avenue stood as reminders for years to come.

Finally, Tom and Margaret split up. Tom Potter, whose drinking had progressed to a point that worried some locals, took off for Florida, and Margaret continued to live and make music in Asbury. Tom's granddaughter recounts the story:

> The decline of Asbury presented citizens with few options. They could stay and struggle to keep their local business afloat, or they could leave and find new ways to survive. As much as they loved each other, Tom and Margaret found themselves on different sides of the line. After 10 years of blissful marriage, the obstacles that came with two decades between them finally took their toll. Margaret was a bright young woman, deeply rooted in the town, and enthusiastic about Asbury's comeback. Tom was alone with no family members still in the state,

approaching retirement, suffering health problems, and now unemployed. By the next year with what money he had left, his bags were packed and ready to go. No amount of persuasion could change Margaret's mind. They parted ways, each genuinely expecting the other to follow.[81]

They let the lease lapse at the end of October 1970, with the Bruce Springsteen Band playing the penultimate night.

The downtown, already in decline, was decimated as beachgoers, tourists, and shoppers stayed away, and parents told their kids to steer clear of Asbury Park. It did not all happen at once, and Asbury continued to have a musical tradition built around clubs. The Stone Pony opened in 1973 and Bruce, Southside Johnny, and many, many others continued to play live music. If much of the Jersey Shore scene fostered cover bands rather than experimentation, the clubs still provided the places where scenes could develop. Sonny Kenn captures the dynamic: "Clubs always seem to be the place where music—and when you talk about a folk tradition, because rock music really is folk, it's not passed down by written notes, it's passed down by word of mouth, and records, and hearing, which is a traditional way of music carrying on—those places that allowed that to happen become fewer and fewer, or situations become tighter and tighter, pretty soon the candle dwindles and blows out. Till some other spark lights it up again, and it starts over."[82]

6 • "DRUMS ALONG THE HUDSON"

The Hoboken Sound

As the rock 'n' roll business consolidated and corporatized in the 1970s, with touring bands playing fewer and larger venues, the rock world was now one of stars and fans. Fans were consumers of distant and larger-than-life rock icons. The system worked, at least for the majority of rock fans who listened to album-oriented rock on FM radio and bought tickets to the closest arena months in advance of touring rock acts. And the system worked for the record companies that churned out product and earned their profits. But by the mid-1970s, pockets of discontent arose across the rock world. If Beatlemania in 1964 had unleashed a generational id, the punk rock that blasted out of CBGB beginning in 1974 trickled out its influence much more slowly. It is difficult to remember now, but the Ramones were revolutionary. Their look was revolutionary. Their sound was unlike anything on the airwaves at the time. They were either feared as a threat or maligned and dismissed as a joke.

It did not all begin with the Ramones. In Detroit, the Stooges and MC5 had already pioneered a rampaging rock sound, and the connection to the White Panther Party had established Detroit as a scene. In Cleveland, the Electric Eels and others had been toiling in local obscurity. Even in New York, Suicide had already signaled something new, as a bridge from the 1960s' days of the Fillmore East and the Velvet Underground's tenure at Andy Warhol's Factory. But the New York scene took off when the Ramones and others established residency at CBGB on the Bowery in New York in 1974. Although the musicians were hardly oblivious to the marketplace and the lure of rock stardom, what distinguished the scene there was the commitment to experimentation and making music that felt real and authentic in an era when rock music was increasingly complex and produced, distant and pretentious.

After New York came London, and punk rock became an international scourge and phenomenon in 1977. The tabloids screamed about "the filth and the fury," and music fans around the world took away an ethos that had become alien to the bloated, corporate rock showbiz world: do it yourself (DIY). The Sex Pistols may have set out to destroy rock 'n' roll, but they inspired young people to pick up instruments and form bands wherever they went and whenever a major media agency reported on their threat to civilization. In the late 1970s, young people in small pockets around the world began to form bands and scenes in a loosely connected network. In Hoboken, New Jersey, a scene thrived throughout the 1980s and into the 1990s, bringing independent, underground music to the local community and a national audience.

An unlikely spot for a musical renaissance, Hoboken was "the misused back alley of some other, better place," a place where "each neighborhood has its own weather."[1] Never much of a place to call home, from "its earliest conception, Hoboken was a place mainly to get into and then out of again."[2] Like most urban areas in the United States in the 1970s, the Mile Square City had seen better days, no longer enjoying the status of a major port city, as it had since World War I when more than 3 million soldiers passed through on their way to the European front. Shipbuilding and manufacturing jobs were plentiful through the mid-twentieth century, as the American industrial economy expanded.

In an all-too-familiar tale, manufacturing left for cheaper land and non-union labor, shipbuilding moved overseas, as the housing stock deteriorated and the population fled for the suburbs. The once-fabled port, the site of *On the Waterfront*, became all but abandoned by the 1970s, as shippers moved to deeper harbors. Hoboken "had the lowest per capita income, highest unemployment, the lowest education levels," in the county, according to Robert Foster, the executive director of the Hoboken Historical Museum. "Everything was bad, especially morale."[3]

As real estate prices crumbled, however, new groups, particularly immigrants from Puerto Rico, arrived. Among the new arrivals were young bohemian types, priced out of New York, or simply looking for something a bit outside the denseness of Manhattan but still within striking distance via the PATH train. The young immigrants to Hoboken built a scene that served as a satellite to the rock world of Manhattan, a node on the national and international underground rock network, and a self-contained musical home.

Across the United States, in the wake of punk's explosion in New York and London, new music scenes arose, part of what Michael Azerrad calls "a cultural underground railroad."[4] Azerrad builds his brilliant story of the "American indie underground" around some important bands and their record labels—from Black Flag and the Minutemen to Fugazi and Beat Happening. The bands are important, indeed. But those bands arose within scenes that built up locally, with an infrastructure of clubs, zines, record stores, and hangouts for the people to gather and form those bands and labels. Hoboken nurtured its own scene, while also helping to create the "cultural underground railroad" for touring bands.

Although it is always dangerous to ascribe origins to one particular moment or place, perhaps the Hoboken scene begins with Maxwell's—the tavern that became the home for dozens of local bands and an iconic stop for touring indie bands. Its co-owner, Steve Fallon, remembers scouring the city for a space and noticing that Maxwell's Tavern, at the corner of Hoboken's main drag Washington Street at Eleventh, was closed whenever he went by. "I finally found the owner and asked, 'When the fuck are you open?' He said, 'Between shift changes at the Maxwell House coffee plant down the road: 5:30 to 6:30 a.m. and 11:30 p.m. to 12:30 a.m.' The factory workers would have a shot and a beer in between shifts."[5] Fallon, his brother, sister, and her husband bought the building in 1978 for $67,000. When the Fallon family purchased the tavern, cleaned it up a bit, and began booking bands, the locals who were there for the cheap brownstones had a place to play and "word quickly spread—about the club, about Hoboken's cheap rents and easy commute to the city—and musicians and artists started moving in, which in turn sparked the city's eventual gentrification."[6]

With a population under 50,000 Hoboken experienced decline in a peculiar sort of way in the 1970s. Having escaped the large-scale upheaval and riots of Newark and Asbury Park, Hoboken had what might be called a genteel decline. "I was afraid to walk by there by myself back then," the Hoboken native Alice Genese remembers. "On any given day, there'd be people crawling on the sidewalk, falling down drunk, starting fights. It was scary when you were a young girl." The dozens of bars along the fourteen blocks of Washington Street marked the city as tough, working-class territory. But, although it had always had its share of corruption, crime, and prostitution, the city was hardly devastated. "I grew up a tough kid with eyes in the back of my head," Genese recalls. "When I grew up there, this city was very blue-collar and people were very hard-working, but there was a lot of love. Neighbors watched out for each other's children. People took care of one another."[7] Rents were incredibly cheap as the housing stock deteriorated, with heat and hot water often lacking. Apartments above Maxwell's went for $55 a month.

The neighborhood was perhaps "sketchy," but it was not exactly dangerous. Therefore, for those who wanted urban life and creativity but maybe were not ready to brave the maelstrom of 1970s New York, Hoboken was welcoming, despite the ever-present "scent of burned coffee" from the plant down the road.[8] James Mastro, who joined the Bongos when he arrived in Hoboken (and moved into an apartment above the club), recalled, "In a weird way, it was easier to tell my parents I was moving to Hoboken than to New York."[9] Glenn Morrow, who moved into a six-room flat across from the coffee factory for $65 a month, remembers, "Hoboken was more innocent than the East Village, not quite as debauched. We were suburban kids who fell in love with the third Velvet Underground record."[10] In fact, to many of the new inhabitants, "Hoboken felt safe and worlds away from Manhattan," more like the 1950s towns they remembered from childhood or television.[11] Richard Barone remembers arriving in Hoboken, "It was as if the train had transported me not only far from Manhattan, but far from the current year as well, turning the clock back 20 years or so in those 20 minutes. A total time warp. The town that time forgot . . ."[12]

"A friend of mine came to my apartment," recalled Glenn Morrow. "She said, 'There's a bar around the corner that wants to have live original music of a modern variety.' I was stunned. The only room we knew about at the time in New Jersey that would have us was out in Dover. Now, here was a place to play right where we were living."[13] Morrow had put together a band called "a," and went to see if they could rehearse in the back and play some gigs at the tavern: "I gave Steve Fallon a cassette tape. He listened and said, 'Come back Saturday night, you're going to play three sets.'"[14] The day of his first gig, Morrow's car was stolen and he performed his brand-new song "Someone Stole My Car" that very night.[15] The "a" band built on the influences that were bubbling up from the underground in the late 1970s, as their *Village Voice* ad seeking an "inventive" guitarist signified—"Talking Heads, TV [Television], Reggae, Eno." Richard Barone answered the ad and connected with Morrow, Rob Norris, and Frank Giannini.[16] After "a" disbanded, Morrow founded the Individuals and Rage to Live, and the others went on to create the Bongos, eventually taking on guitarist James Mastro.

Maxwell's started booking bands, at first without even a stage or a sound system, eventually setting a stage in the back room that held two hundred people. "It wasn't really a rock club," according to Will Rigby of the dB's. "It was a working-class bar with bare lightbulbs on the ceiling, and when we played, some of the patrons laughed at us. We didn't sound like Bob Seger or whatever was on the radio."[17] Almost instantly, a scene grew up around the club. "Applying a fresh coat of paint, polishing up the back-room bar, and adding a sound mixer/DJ booth, the place was transformed," according to Richard Barone. "Our practice sound system and the casual air of community that existed at the beginning remained throughout Maxwell's heyday years. It was rare, then and now, to experience a venue where the separation between performer and audience was less distinct. The lines blurred. Because the newly built stage was low to the ground, and the room so small (200 people was jam-packed), the synergy was palpable. What happened off the stage was often just as entertaining as what happened on."[18]

Everywhere a new subcultural scene develops, all the ingredients are already there but one. It takes just a spark to ignite. "The day we opened," according to Steve Fallon, "we were still trying to get hinges on the front door. People were literally walking over us to get into the bar. Hoboken was ready."[19] As the scene grew, musicians and bohemians flocked to the town for its music, including members of Yo La Tengo, who "wanted to move to a place where we could live a little better. And where we could walk to a club"— and where they could share a whole house for under $200 a month.[20] Because of the cheap rents, artists could afford to make art. "For people to really be creative they can't be consumed every minute by how they are going to make money to pay high rents," remembers Karyn Kuhl. "It was an organic music scene because people could be more relaxed about that."[21]

Soon, bands like the Individuals, the Bongos, the dB's, the Feelies, and Yo La Tengo became staples on a burgeoning scene that developed an international reputation for "The Hoboken Sound." Probably a misnomer, a product of fevered A&R dreams, a journalist's hook to create a story, similar to what real estate agents do to create a desirable neighborhood, the Hoboken

The Individuals at Maxwell's, 1980. (Courtesy of Jim Testa.)

Sound involved jangly guitars that could go poppy or edgy depending on the band. One scenester sums up, "Bands from Hoboken were poppy but slightly weird. Yo La Tengo became synonymous with Hoboken, which seems right, because they had beautiful songs and weirdness happening at the same time."[22]

It is a story repeated throughout the history of rock 'n' roll: one band creates a stir, and the business people descend, gobbling up every local band, searching for the next big thing, the "New Liverpool."[23] Hoboken had its moment, but never a big one. That is just as well because those big moments never really amounted to much. The grunge scene of Seattle in the 1990s was emblematic. After Nirvana vaulted to the top of the charts with *Nevermind* in 1991, the locusts arrived. Asbury Park in the 1970s had its day, after Bruce conquered the world and the Stone Pony became mecca. But in 1985 the local Channel 5 aired an hour narrated by Bob O'Brien on "The Hoboken Sound" that tried to capture the spirit of the music scene.

The Hoboken scene rests on a different level as a scene that never quite burst into mainstream consciousness but had a good twenty-year run (maybe even more) as a vital musical hub producing vibrant local music and channeling rock music from all over the world as touring artists dropped in. In the 1980s, there were similar scenes, all with their own local inflections, across the continent, in places such as Athens, Georgia, Minneapolis, the San Francisco Bay Area, Lawrence, Kansas, Vancouver, British Columbia, and many others. As mainstream rock radio stayed with the album-oriented rock that had emerged in the 1970s, college radio across the country created another set of links for new sounds to spread. MTV's inauguration in 1981 placed bright-colored clothing, wild hairdos, and bouncy beats at the center of pop music.

The A&R reps came and they found some fodder. Some of the Hoboken bands fit what they were looking for—clean, bouncy, fun, with hooks. Others were a bit too edgy and dissonant for the mainstream music business to take a chance on, but a number of them found their niche in the emerging indie scene network. No band broke through to superstardom the way Bruce Springsteen had from Asbury Park, but many bands still play music, often together with the same old friends, decades later.

The Bongos, with *Tiger Beat* good looks, the requisite teased and gelled hair, not even afraid of a little eyeliner, had the look and sound of the next big thing, with powerful hooks, jangly rhythms, and crafty lyrics. Signed to RCA after several singles and their debut album *Drums Along the Hudson*, the Bongos went the way of most indie bands who jumped at a major label offer. Their next album sank, in an era (just like most every era) when the corporate music business was afraid to miss out on what was happening but was too tame, too dependent on finding an exact copy of the last big thing, to actually expend any capital promoting fresh sounding music. Matt Pinfield, a DJ and aspiring indie rock musical influencer, fell in love with "their vigor and visceral delivery of the pop side street." Pinfield's influence could only arrive after Nirvana's album overturned all the rock business conventions, when he became the host of MTV's *120 Minutes* in 1995. In the 1980s, however, "In an era where great indie records had no chance of breaking through to the mainstream, I was shouting from the tops of the buildings telling people . . . 'Listen to this! The world is changing!'"[24] But others thought the band itself had sold out, so that, although the video for "Numbers with Wings," was nominated for an MTV Video Music Award for Best Direction, *Trouser Press* deemed the album mostly "adequate but dispensable."[25]

The rock critic Robert Palmer summarized the dilemma facing musicians in a 1987 review, outlining how the indie scene had "split into two mutually exclusive camps, one emphasizing intensity and artistic integrity, the other

JERSEY BEAT
New Jersey's New-Music Nexus

Vol. 1 No. 2   April - May 82

POP! Go The   50¢

...BONGOS!

Jersey Beat no. 2, April–May 1982. (Courtesy of Jim Testa.)

willing to compromise in order to reach a broader audience. The Bongos were signed to a major record label and proceeded to make slick, overproduced records which vitiated the raw vitality the group had originally displayed. They failed to achieve major commercial success, and they lost some of their original fans in the process."[26]

The Cucumbers, led by Deena Shoshkes and Jon Fried turned out power pop that was unabashedly commercial and listener-friendly. Having met in college, they began to make music together, including busking through Europe and landing in Hoboken in 1981, and playing their first gig at Maxwell's opening for the Individuals before the end of the year. For their first show, their friends tossed cucumber slices. Afterward Fallon warned them, "Make sure your friends don't come back with cucumbers, because the smell of cucumbers and old beer is awful."[27]

By the middle of the decade, the couple was married and videos of their song "My Boyfriend" and a cover of "All Shook Up" were getting MTV airplay, with *Rolling Stone* calling their work "unpretentious boy/girl bop . . . as fresh as it is irresistible."[28] The band even got the approval of Robert Christgau in his influential *Village Voice Consumer Guide*, where he called "My Boyfriend" "a girl-group masterstroke for a feminist age" and concluded about Deena Shoshkes, "The more I hear of her vivid sweetness the more sexy and unprecedented it seems."[29] The critic Jon Pareles writing in the *New York Times* similarly found their songs "winsome on top, sinewy down below. . . . There's a danger that such bare-faced songs could turn cute or cynical, but the Cucumbers rarely succumb. More often, they're both direct and artful— and as sincere as a smart pop band gets."[30]

No band left a greater legacy than the Feelies, who by 1978 were being called "The Best Underground Band" by the *Village Voice*. The Feelies rejected the star-making machine and even pulled back when their universally well-reviewed debut album *Crazy Rhythms* came out in 1980 on Stiff America Records. Most obviously influenced by the Velvet Underground and the Stooges' "I Wanna Be Your Dog," the band churned out dreamy and hypnotic, yet melodic, dirges. The band was attracted to Maxwell's because "it was the complete opposite of what we had experienced in New York. It was more lowkey and we found it more genuine and much more suitable for the band."[31] They faced the dilemma of how much to grasp for the mainstream version of success, which all rockers were supposed to be in it for. After the success of *Crazy Rhythms*, the band shut down its public profile for five years (later they took another seventeen-year break).

As they told one disbelieving interviewer when they reemerged in the mid-1980s, "Well, we don't mind being a cult band, all our favorite bands are cult bands."[32] On the other hand, "bands that we considered our peers were signed to major labels. It kind of seemed like that situation where you gotta keep moving up," according to Glenn Mercer. In 1985, Steve Fallon branched out from Maxwell's to start the Coyote Records label in order to release local artists, including 1985's aptly titled compilation *Luxury Condos Coming to Your Neighborhood Soon*. Members of the Feelies had recorded for Coyote with their side projects because of their relationship with Fallon: "It felt really comfortable to us. It was just basically a one-man operation and just real good communication between us and the people there."[33] The band itself signed with Coyote, but that label had a deal with A&M Records, which though major, had a slightly more personal feel. As Glenn Mercer explains, "They operated, it seemed at least to us, like an independent label would: kind of small, close-knit, almost a family type of atmosphere."[34] But, as happens all too often, that label was bought by another, the people whom the Feelies knew were suddenly gone, and the band was adrift.

The scene was not just a collection of bands. Maxwell's formed the hub, but a whole constellation of other institutions grew up to make the scene happen. The *New York Rocker*, for which Glenn Morrow and Ira Kaplan wrote, published coverage to spread the word, especially their November 1982 issue on Hoboken, "Bands across the Water: Exploring a Model Pop Community." The magazine, and zines like Jim Testa's *Jersey Beat*, also provided a gestalt, a sense of the bigger picture, as they situated the Hoboken scene within a larger universe of indie rock that was being built. Named as a pun on "Mersey Beat," the zine was produced in typical DIY fashion. "I wrote it on a manual typewriter, cut and pasted the stories and pictures onto typewriter paper, and had it run off at a printing shop that did business cards and stationery," Jim Testa recalled. "Then I brought the pages home and stapled them together myself. I interviewed more bands and went to a lot of shows."[35]

Bar/None Records was founded in 1986 by Tom Prendergast, who released an album by Glenn Morrow's latest band Rage to Live and brought him on as a partner. Bar/None became an important local label, just as with clubs, zines, college radio, and the other infrastructure of the indie music world, local musicians, fans, and entrepreneurs took to making their own institutions to make the scene happen. The label released albums by They Might Be Giants, Yo La Tengo, Freedy Johnston, and dozens of indie artists over the next three decades. Situated in a beautiful 1889 industrial landmark, the Hoboken Land Building, near the downtown post office, Bar/None ran in typical indie DIY fashion. Mary Marcus became its first intern and employee: "I called Glenn and said I wanted to be an intern. He asked me what that was. I said I would work for free. He told me to come in." When she arrived, the phone rang, she was told to answer it. "I did. It was for Glenn. I took a message. Glenn came in. I gave him the message. He hired me."[36]

Kate Jacobs recorded for the label in the 1990s, and noted the down and dirty methods. "Glenn had a reputation as a frugal maker of records," she recalled. "He had a favorite saying that we often quoted in our recording sessions over the years: 'Is the amp on? Is there a mic near it? Roll tape!'" The recording artist also participated in all the dirty work necessary to build the scene. "I commuted to my day job on the PATH, and when my album came out, I would often stop at the Bar/None office on my way home to help with copying press releases, drilling holes in promo jewel cases, stuffing jiffy bags, stamping, and carrying boxfuls of packages to the PO," Jacobs recalled. "I spent many afternoons sitting on the floor with Tom, stickering and stamping mountains of jiffy bags going to press and radio."[37]

The labels distributed nationally through a growing network of independent distributors that got the records out to DJs on college radio stations and local record stores. Hoboken, thus, had a full-fledged musical scene in the mid-1980s, just as other scenes were springing up across the country. Glenn Morrow worked with the network of distributors: "In the early 1980s a new group of independent distributors came into being as consumers discovered the latest releases from new wave and punk rock record labels as well as artists on European labels. . . . Someone was always going out of business which made labels fearful of putting all their eggs in one basket."[38] Local record stores stocked the discs, and in downtown Hoboken, Billy Ryan and Bar/None's Tom Prendergast opened Pier Platters, an important place for fans to find music from the growing international indie music scene.[39]

Hoboken, perhaps unique in local scenes, had a tight relationship with bands from other similar local scenes. Many bands, especially those that came from similar scenes, made Maxwell's a second home. Ohio's Human Switchboard became practically a local band. There seemed to be a special connection to the Athens, Georgia, scene, which produced similarly quirky and idiosyncratic bands that combined pop and avant-garde sensibilities. When Pylon played Maxwell's three times in 1980, they informed the locals to watch out for an even better band on its way—R.E.M. Peter Buck from R.E.M. eventually bought an air conditioner for the club's back room. The Minneapolis bands Hüsker Dü and the Replacements loved the club. Hüsker Dü's Bob Mould moved from Minneapolis to Hoboken in 1989 after his band broke up because that's where Maxwell's and Steve Fallon were.

The Replacements specialized in legendary, drunken train-wreck shows wherever they went, and Maxwell's was no exception. Jim DeRogatis recounts their first visit in 1983, "After a great if messy set, most of the band left the stage, but leader Paul Westerberg wanted to keep going. A few punks in the audience wearing mohawks and leather jackets hopped onstage, Westerberg sat behind the drums, and they played 'Louie Louie' for another 20 minutes. Replacements, indeed."[40] Steve Fallon remembers their appearances fondly, "The Replacements loved Maxwell's. Tommy Stinson brought his mother. They never had a bad show here. Maybe because they knew I'd stay up until 5 a.m. and drink with them."[41] "There was one Replacements show when it got so hot chairs actually melted," Todd Abramson recalls of another legendary set. "It was discovered afterward that the attendance clicker had broken, and they'd let in something like 380 people. Capacity was 200."[42]

The worlds of musicians, critic, promoter, and the like intertwined. So Ira Robbins began as a writer, was hired to do sound for Maxwell's (even though he claims not to have known how to do sound), and then founded the stalwart Hoboken band Yo La Tengo.[43] Glenn Morrow similarly came from the *New York Rocker* to his bands in Hoboken to his partnership in Bar/None Records. "Hoboken had a very collaborative scene, of bands producing other band's albums, designing each other's t-shirts and tour posters, getting each other on shows," according to Richard Barone. "We were all involved with each other, and Maxwell's was at the center of it all. It was a very non-aggressive venue that didn't impose a style on bands or audiences. You didn't have to be anyone but yourself at Maxwell's, you were good enough, and that inspired creativity."[44]

The indie rock world was more open about gender and sexual roles than the mainstream world. Punk scenes in London, New York, and Los Angeles, for example, were heavily influenced by strong women, and fluid sexual identities were welcome, though not always explicitly. The scenes were not without sexism and discrimination, but in comparison to the rest of American society, they were ideal places to explore and find oneself in a supportive environment, especially for those struggling with their identity. Bob Mould writes: "On June 23 [1984] we played our very first show at the great Hoboken club Maxwell's, which soon became a standard stop on the indie rock circuit. The club owner was a very gregarious fellow named Steve Fallon. Steve's gaydar went off on me immediately, and I finally had somebody in a big city who knew gay, who knew I was gay, and who I could learn from. Maxwell's

Ira Kaplan of Yo La Tengo, on the left, and Steve Fallon at Maxwell's, 1984. (Courtesy of Jim Testa.)

was gay-friendly, but it wasn't a gay bar. It was just a scene that happened to have gay people in it."[45] Richard Barone remembers, with some annoyance, how Fallon would always greet him with "Hey faggot."[46] "Maxwell's had no particular sexual identity," according to Fallon. "Yes, I was out. But I wasn't your typical fag. Everyone who worked at Maxwell's was a little eccentric. That was the beauty of it."[47] Barone recalls, "The club was extremely bisexual. The same way a president affects the tone of a country, the owner of a club affects the clientele. Who did I sleep with? Everyone."[48]

Similarly, with the involvement of women, the Hoboken scene was hardly perfect, but definitely more open. Too many bands had their token woman bass player. But in the indie world of the 1980s, women began to take full citizenship in rock 'n' roll, expanding on the pioneering punks of the 1970s and paving the way for the Riot Grrrl movement and indie explosion of woman-dominated music in the 1990s. Gut Bank, which had a much harder sound than most local bands, was nevertheless welcomed. Composed of three young women and one man, the band also pushed against the gender norms of the rock world, even the indie rock world that seemed to relegate women to bass player status. "Steve Fallon really took us under his wing and was so support-ive, even though we were just kids, really," Alice Genese remembers.[49] The guitarist Karyn Kuhl adds, "We were a noisy, post-punk band that didn't really fit the so-called 'Hoboken Sound.' But we did have three born-and-raised Hobokenites—Alice, Tia and Mike—which in essence made us the most Hoboken of all Hoboken bands."[50] But the whole infrastructure of the local scene supported the band, including Bill Ryan at Pier Platters. Alice Genese remembers how they "helped foster young talent in a way that I think is rare to find. . . . And especially as [young women] . . . we were embraced and wel-comed and supported."[51] Janet Wygal, who played in the Individuals and other bands, remembers the scene as "still pretty male dominated," but "a very safe environment" to explore and be accepted as a musician,[52] even if it did have—"this is a nightclub after all"—only one women's toilet, with a line often longer than the line to get into the show.[53]

It is nearly impossible to find a complaint by a musician about Maxwell's. It started with Steve Fallon and extended to Todd Abramson, who took over the booking in the mid-1980s and partial ownership in the mid-1990s. "Todd was like my younger brother," according to Fallon. "We had the same tastes. More importantly, we didn't do the five-band, screw-you, open-a-calendar-and-write-a-name-down thing. We wanted the bills to have some coherence."[54] Universally, bands appreciated the way they were treated at the club.

Bands continued to play at the club long after they could sell out larger venues. "When the band first came here, perhaps they weren't that well-known yet," Abramson notes. "But we treated them well. And they remem-bered that. And then the next tour, when they were playing larger rooms, you know, let's go back to that place; they really took care of us."[55] Fallon knew from his days managing bands how different Maxwell's was from the norm: "I think the bands could actually really feel comfortable—we *tried* to make them feel comfortable. Whenever you went on tour with bands—I also man-aged bands—you'd walk into a club, no one would greet you, you'd kind of stand around for an hour, and then the cranky, hungover soundman would come and basically throw shit on the stage. So we really made an effort not to be that way. . . . I think it all comes down to that they were returning to us what we were giving to them."[56] Imagine the difference it made for a touring band "that had lived on peanut butter sandwiches for weeks" to be "treated to a great meal from the kitchen (Fettuccine Maxwell's a specialty) and free-flowing John Courage Ale on tap," as Jim DeRogatis noted. "And for years,

Karyn Kuhl of Gutbank at Maxwell's, circa mid-1980s. (Courtesy of Jim Testa.)

groups that didn't have a place to crash were invited to stay in an apartment upstairs."[57]

It was clear that Fallon and Abramson cared about the music and took "a curatorial approach . . . that respected the intelligence of the audience & performers alike,"[58] and the cultivation of the scene. It might have been the only club in the world that actually fed the bands, even the opening acts. "You could tell they really cared about music there," remembers one musician. "The opening bands were always carefully selected. The bills were never overcrowded. The set times were not too early or too late. The vibe and atmosphere was always perfect."[59] One local writer concluded, "Steve and Todd had the vision to imagine a place that would treat musicians with respect and hospitality, pay them fairly and treat them with dignity. That was rare back in the Eighties and Nineties; it's virtually unheard of today."[60]

Fans loved the club because it embodied the collaborative spirit of the indie scene. "Maxwell's was less about trying to make a scene, and it was just a place to hear great music," said Kaplan. "It had the feeling of being more of an adjunct to our basements."[61] Bands ate in the front-room restaurant with everyone else, and they had to make their way through the crowd to get to the stage. The clientele were mostly "lifer music freaks" who were treated, like the musicians, with respect in a club that was "less concerned with 'hip' and being pretentious."[62] The vibe, all too rare in the indie world and especially absent in New York, created an "intangible bond between the bands and the club itself and the people who came."[63] The zine writer Gerard Cosley, who saw bands in hundreds of clubs around the world, concluded "Maxwell's felt like a place that was owned & staffed by persons who thought the players and paying customers were friends and peers. As opposed to, y'know, targets & tools in the all-important struggle to sell more beer. . . . It was a genuinely big deal to see live music in a space where every single person on the premises was glad to be there."[64]

The writers Jim Testa and Jim DeRogatis started as young eager fans and aspiring journalists who also ended up in various bands—and their stories illustrate how the scene created a community, but also shaped individual identities, especially for young people coming of age.

In 1980, unemployed, trying to find his way after graduating college with a degree in journalism, "with very little idea of what he wanted to do with his life," Testa, "wandered into a small bar in Hoboken to see a band called the Bongos." It turned out to be the moment that changed his life. Maxwell's "wasn't dark and dangerous and fairly forbidding like CBGB. It didn't have velvet ropes and snooty doormen like Danceteria and the Mudd Club. It was like this magic little alternate reality were everyone knew everyone else, and everyone there was fabulous." Miraculously and inexplicably, Testa found his home, starting with a chat with Ira Kaplan and then a meeting with the band—something you could never do at an arena rock show unless you were a groupie. Soon, Testa was playing softball and bowling with the gang of Maxwell's regulars. Along the way, he toured with bands, "slept on floors and couches and met musicians and made friends all across this country, in more cities than I can remember. I've shared a tour van with the Pink Lincolns in Florida, rocked to the Queers in Eugene, Oregon, dined on the Mission District's best burritos with Pansy Division in San Francisco, watched a Cubs game at Wrigley Field with Ben Weasel, discussed Kerouac with Mike Watt, traded quips with Dr. Frank, shared a stage with Ted Leo, and seen the Wrens play a Hoboken loft naked." Testa built a life résumé that would have seemed impossible to dream of as an aspiring reporter. And he concluded: "None of that happens if I didn't walk into Maxwell's to see the Bongos back in 1980."[65]

Jim DeRogatis shares a similar story that begins with him sneaking into Maxwell's "as a precocious 18-year-old in 1982." There he "really learned what it means to be a fan—to love music so much that you can sooner imagine going without food or oxygen." Although punk was "supposed to tear down the artificial walls between the artists and the audience, it never really did," especially for an aspiring rock critic from Hudson Catholic Regional High School in Jersey City. "You always had to worry about fitting in at C.B.G.B., just as you had to wait to be chosen to get past the velvet rope at Danceteria or the Mudd Club, and just as you always had to fret about being 'cool enough' to belong at pretty much any other club. That never was the case at Maxwell's, for musicians or for fans." At Maxwell's, DeRogatis "saw so many life-changing shows . . . : countless gigs by local heroes such as the Feelies, the Bongos, the dB's, Yo La Tengo and Sonic Youth, as well as performances by touring acts like the Replacements, Hüsker Dü, R.E.M., the Minutemen, Robyn Hitchcock, Alex Chilton, Wire . . . I could go on, and on, and on." And from there, he, like Testa, launched a career as a journalist that took him to the farthest reaches of the rock world.[66]

Melissa Pierson, another young writer, but not a rock world scenester, similarly understood the tremendous and serendipitous good fortune of being a regular at the club. "You knew you were witnessing the height that art was wont to reach," she wrote in her memoir *The Place You Love Is Gone*, "and you understood it, every microscopically thin layer of intention sitting on another." Watching bands at Maxwell's "was like having Mozart come to play a little something in your living room."[67] Pierson's memoir laments the passing of that special time, but she eloquent depicts how "progress hits home." In fact, Maxwell's itself provided the seed for its own demise. For, at the very time that Steve Fallon was looking for property, so were developers and speculators. The very cheap rents that brought bohemian youth also led landlords to begin to convert rental stock to condos. A series of tenement fires swept through the city during the club's early years, as arson became a vehicle to displace the working poor from increasingly valuable properties. By the early 1980s, "real estate offices appeared like mushrooms in wet woods."[68]

Successive waves of gentrification completely remodeled the city. As early as 1987, the Cucumbers, in a song that Christgau considered "the best song ever written about gentrification or Hoboken," were singing of "My Town" with a mixture of irony and wistful nostalgia.[69]

My town, the sign says it's home of Frank Sinatra . . .

There were bars all along the river
Back then they called them watering caves
Now it's just a piece of somebody's money
Now it's just a piece of somebody's money
In my town, my town

Is this the same
Place it used to be
Was there ever
A time when land was free
Don't you want
Don't you want to live here? . . .

This lovely town
Has killed a few souls
It may yet do

Away with a few more
Don't you want
Don't you want to live here?[70]

Jim DeRogatis recalls, "Throughout the period that I covered the city as a beat reporter for the *Jersey Journal* in the mid to late '80s, it was a vibrant mix of Italian and hispanic working-class immigrants and younger bohemians driven out of Manhattan by escalating rents. It was a great place to work, live, and create—too great, as it turned out."[71] By the 1990s, Hoboken was already becoming unrecognizable. Fallon sold the club, and its new owners turned it into a trendy brewpub. Thankfully, Abramson and his partners bought the club back, and Maxwell's had another good, long run.

Richard Barone captured the slow, inevitable end of the scene: "As Hoboken grew, gentrified, and its rents increased, the innocence and unique characteristics fell away one by one. Instead of mom-and-pop stores, the chains came in. Sidewalks seemed suddenly overcrowded. The blue-collar families were replaced with a new wave of aggressive professionals; artists and musicians were squeezed out to make room. Now, rowdy sports bars overtook Washington Street as weekend traffic and parking became unbearable."[72] "I realized it was over," Karyn Kuhl remembers, "when I couldn't go out of the house on a weekend night without having to deal with packs of 'drink till you puke in the street' types."[73]

Maxwell's closed for good in July 2013, with a series of sold-out retrospective shows by the old stalwarts, including Yo La Tengo (who had played yearly Hanukkah shows), the Feelies, and the Individuals. Fittingly, "a" and the Bongos played the final show, with numerous guests from Maxwell's scene. The *New York Times* noted upon the club's closing, "But most of Maxwell's neighborhood has long since been taken over by luxury high-rise buildings named for the thrumming factories that they replaced."[74] The old Maxwell House factory, source of the famous odor of Hoboken, was converted into multimillion-dollar condos. Construction was under way as Abramson decided to close down the club—not because he had to financially, but because the time just seemed right to let go. "The place I knew is gone; the place that retained history's marks is gone," Melissa Pierson wrote.[75] The scene had come and gone.

CONCLUSION

Making the Scene in the Twenty-First Century

There are so many other scenes that have nurtured New Jersey-ans' love of music over the years. If you frequented the Meadowbrook in the 1940s, where Frank Sinatra, Tommy Dorsey, Louis Prima, and all the great big bands of the era played, no doubt you are filled with nostalgic memories. Or you might have listened to Charlie Barnet play "Pompton Turnpike," the tune dedicated to the club on the live show on CBS radio between 1937 and 1941, "Coming to you from Frank Dailey's Meadowbrook, Route 23, the Pompton Turnpike in Cedar Grove." Or maybe you danced there when it was briefly resurrected as a new-wave disco in the 1980s.[1]

Somebody needs to write a book about the house concert scenes in New Jersey, especially the extraordinary Live @ Drew's in Ringwood. Since 1997 Drew Eckmann has hosted artists such as Robert Gordon, Alejandro Escovedo, Kinky Friedman, the Blasters, and Graham Parker (who has played 13 times) for over 250 living-room concerts at his house on Cupsaw Lake.[2]

If you hung out at the Dirt Club in the 1980s, you and your friends have some stories to tell. The music at Albert Hall in the Pine Barrens of southern New Jersey, a folk, bluegrass, and country scene that dates to the 1950s, is beginning to get the documentation and analysis that it deserves.[3] Since 1975, students at Rutgers University have staged the New Jersey Folk Festival.[4] The Jersey Shore has a long tradition of cover bands that have their own

fan bases and even make a living performing live music.[5] The Capitol Theatre in Passaic, home to legendary rock shows in the 1970s, deserves its own
book, if only to capture the vibrant life of the folks who toiled behind the
scenes. Newark's jazz scenes have been captured nicely in a series of books
by Barbara J. Kukla.[6]

I was sorry not to write about the 1980s–1990s punk rock scene at City
Gardens in Trenton in this book. But the magisterial *No Slam Dancing, No
Stage Diving, No Spikes: An Oral History of the Legendary City Gardens*, by
Amy Yates Wuelfing and Steven DiLodovico, and the documentary *Riot on
the Dance Floor: The Story of Randy Now and City Gardens* (2014) really cover
it all so well.[7] I would have just ended up stealing their material.

New Brunswick's scene, particularly its tradition of basement shows, has
also had a lasting and ongoing influence. The Rutgers University Special Collections and University Archives, founded by Christine A. Lutz, the New Jersey regional studies librarian, and Frank Bridges, a doctoral student at Rutgers, now has an exciting and growing archive of flyers, zines, and recordings.[8]
David Urbano's VLH Films is chronicling the scene in a new documentary,
Noisy Basements and Bars: New Brunswick, New Jersey's Scene within a Scene.[9]

I conclude this book with a brief tour around my neighborhood where
music scenes proliferate. My town is by no means perfect, but people move
here because the community expresses a set of values that we share. Histori-
cally biracial, the town is still beset with too much segregation and racial
inequality, and the long-standing character of the town is severely threatened
by rising costs as the people who would traditionally have moved here can no
longer afford it. But when it works, it really works. And music is central to that.

I can wake up any morning and start planning my musical day—and I do
not even have to leave the five-mile radius of Montclair, my town of 37,669 in
suburban northern New Jersey, thirteen miles from New York City, with the
slightly obnoxious slogan "Where the Suburbs Meet the City."

If I am feeling particularly lazy, I need only walk a few doors up the block to
Tierney's Tavern, where upstairs the Fabulous Flemtones have been playing on
the last Friday of every month since 1986.[10] While cover bands are not really
my thing, they play a pretty scorching version of "Sultans of Swing." I have seen
countless friends' bands at Tierney's, and my own band plays there regularly
and hosts the annual "Thee Volatiles Punk Rock Holiday Extravaganza."

As many weekends as possible, I stop in for BBQ and blues at Ruthie's, a
tiny place with outdoor seating when weather permits, where I have seen

Charlie Hunter, Bobby Radcliffe, and the local rockabilly favorites the Eugene Chrysler Band more times than I can count.

There are open mics weekly or monthly all over town, at Trend Coffee Shop, Tierney's, and Java Love Coffee Roasting Co., weekly shows through the summer at Montclair Center Stage, other occasional DIY events at 73 See Gallery, the Notes from Home House Concert Series, Creativity Caravan, East Side Mags comic book store—some of them staged through Indie Arts Montclair. These little gatherings incubate new institutions, of which some survive, and others fade out. Some will probably close before this book hits the shelves, but others will arise.

In the mid-1980s, friends gathering regularly to share songs wanted to create a coffeehouse vibe, where they could meet regularly, maybe host traveling artists. They ended up creating a lasting and impressive institution Outpost in the Burbs that connects the music-loving public with local charitable institutions. Hosting shows at the majestic First Congregational Church and the Unitarian Church (where the seats are much more comfortable), the Outpost has presented a variety of Americana, folk, and rock acts. Founded in 1987 as a "non-profit outreach organization dedicated to building community through music, community service, and cultural programs," the Outpost brings in legendary artists such as Judy Collins, Roger McGuinn, and Richie Havens, as well as newer contemporary folk acts. About one hundred volunteers work in the community to put on the shows, which raise money for national and local charities such as Habitat for Humanity, Community Foodbank of New Jersey, and Human Needs Pantry. On Saturdays, Outpost volunteers run a soup kitchen serving one hundred people at the Church of the Epiphany in Orange.[11] Gina Auriemma, the former president of Outpost's board of trustees, claims, "The atmosphere is inviting and cozy. Artists feel like they're members of a big family when they come to perform, and the audience feels the same way. Outpost is more than just a concert series—it's a community."[12]

A number of the local scenes have been created by people gathering together to create music, but also to lend their talents to serve the community. Parents Who Rock (PWR) was founded by Alma Schneider who just wanted to rock again while raising kids. It turns out that the town is filled with people in their thirties and up who have the talent and drive to play, but no longer fantasize about the rock star life (except maybe for those thirty minutes onstage). Staging shows at local venues like Tierney's, the Montclair Art

Museum, or Alma's backyard, PWR raises money for arts programming in the local schools and brings together music-loving boomers (and now millennials) to play covers and originals.

The town has a pretty exceptional jazz legacy. The legendary bassist Reggie Workman has been lending his talents as a teacher to the extraordinary Montclair Academy & Laboratory of Dance, Drum, Drama, run by Maya Milenovic Workman for twenty years. The Grammy Award-winning bassist Christian McBride and the vocalist Melissa Walker host the Montclair Jazz Festival every August in Nishuane Park. The event is run by their Jazz House Kids, a community-based educational organization that has been teaching and spreading the gospel of jazz for fifteen years.[13] If I am in the mood for something more intimate, I can hit Trumpets Jazz Club (since 1985) or the weekly Thursday–night jam session at DLV Lounge, where the owner George Marable has hosted live music since 1972, and where I am likely to see the smiling face of Bruce Tyler behind the drums.[14] Bruce is one of those people who makes the music scenes run, turning up in countless bands and jams, and serving on committees and boards for the (now defunct) Montclair Arts Council, the old Montclair Blues and Jazz Festival, the Montclair African American Heritage Parade and Festival, and much more.

On June 21, the longest day of the year, the town takes part in Make Music Day, with dozens of acts performing throughout the day inside or in front of local stores. Put together by volunteers—many of whom are the same ones who participate in the other events and organizations around town—the event is part of a global celebration of music of the international Fête de la Musique, taking place in 800 cities across 120 countries (including 65 cities in the United States).[15] The event began in France as an undertaking proposed by the minister of culture in 1982. As the event organizers explain, "Completely different from a typical music festival, Make Music is open to anyone who wants to take part. Every kind of musician—young and old, amateur and professional, of every musical persuasion—pours onto streets, parks, plazas, and porches to share their music with friends, neighbors, and strangers."[16]

The local Make Music Day effort is led by Greg Pason, who seems to be involved in every grassroots musical and political happening in town. Greg is the national secretary of the Socialist Party USA and has run for office as the Socialist Party candidate in New Jersey numerous times since the 1990s. He got his start in activism, antiracism, and the DIY art and music scene of

New York's Lower East Side in the late 1980s and is a member of the ABC No Rio collective, for years booking Saturday punk matinees at the now demolished former home on Rivington Street of the "Culture of opposition since 1980."[17] These days you can catch him tooling around town on his yellow bike, connecting, organizing, and building community.

All this just hints at the constant flow of music in this town. And I have not even mentioned the Wellmont Theater, a beautiful venue restored to its majestic 1920s glory a decade ago. I have seen some great shows there, but the place does not seem to actually anchor a scene in town. The space demonstrates how a scene is not about just the bands that come through or the space that hosts them. It seems, so far, that the major corporate booking agencies that have tried to use the venue have not really figured out how to make a go of it. The first ongoing musical development at the Wellmont is the arrival of the Hillsong Church, which holds Sunday morning services. The controversial, music-heavy church has become famous for its ability to attract the famous, including Justin Bieber, who has been spotted around town.[18] The immediate area around the theater is being redeveloped to include a large plaza, other arts spaces, and parking, but it remains to be seen whether the local scene will be able to afford the rising costs of "market-rate" rents in the area.[19]

If I dare cross the border into neighboring towns, I might head to the Oranges where an abundance of venues and scenes have developed over the past generation. Hat City Kitchen was developed by Housing and Neighborhood Development Services (HANDS) Inc., a local nonprofit devoted to making Orange "an inclusive city where people can and do choose to live and work."[20] I can catch some jazz at SuzyQues BBQ. On Tuesday nights, I can hit the blues jam at the Franklin Tavern, where I might catch Bettye Lavette singing with her husband Kevin Kiley, who has been running the jam since 2005.[21] If I want to hear a bar band bang out three sets a night, I can head to Little Falls to the Great Notch Inn, a space so sacred that the state is running its Highway 46 expansion around this 1930s-era venue. And if I want some punk rock, I head to the Clash Bar in Clifton, still my favorite place to play and see bands.

I have to venture just a few short miles more to Maplewood/South Orange to attend Rent Party on the second Friday of every month, situated within a similar community of active music producers and fans of all ages. I have seen some amazing shows at Rent Party, including the local power-pop favorites

Sad About Girls. I discovered the fantastic Karyn Kuhl Band there. And I saw the legendary Wanda Jackson, as Joan Jett passed the bucket around to collect money to fight hunger in the community. Rent Party runs its own community garden and their BackPack Pals program provides lunches for one hundred food-insecure kids weekly. I love Rent Party so much that I will not complain that they decline to book my band again after all these years.

Back in Montclair, the teenagers are continuing the tradition of creating community through music scenes. High school students put on shows monthly through a group called Terry's Serendipity Café. Meeting every Wednesday evening at 6:00 at the boathouse in Edgemont Park throughout the year, the teenagers plan shows every month. Under the tutelage of Ed Carine, who seems to do sound or some other service at every musical event in town, the kids do all the work necessary to create a music scene. The shows take place at the high school amphitheater, local churches, synagogues, and parks, with the kids working the door, keeping the peace, selling concessions, setting up the chairs and sound system, and performing.

Started over twenty years ago by a group of kids shortly after a postal shooting in town left the community traumatized and the adults scared for their children, the kids wanted to take control of their own lives. Ed Carine remembered, "They had an assembly at the high school and they asked the students what they would like." One student answered for a group of them: "What we want is a place to play music and listen to music for us. Not a bar, and no age restrictions." Ed has been teaching the kids how to run the sound board and then tells them to teach the other kids. He teaches, he listens, he offers suggestions, but otherwise, this is the kids' scene. "So they make all the decisions. We meet for an hour a week, talk about how Friday's event went, and what could be improved, what was good that we should keep, and what wasn't good that we should change around."[22]

The more adventurous young people might head over to the Meatlocker, a subterranean punk club as gloriously scummy as any punk club ever. Local and touring acts—punk, hip-hop, spoken word, hardcore, and beyond—perform in a dingy warren of rooms, some showing the metal walls as evidence of the former meat locker. The Meatlocker denizens see a space for the creation of a "a tight-knit community of artists that looked out for themselves and others."[23]

There are rumors of shows as far back as the 1980s, and bands have been rehearsing in the space for years. Peter August stumbled into the place while on leave from the military in the late 1990s: "I was home in NJ visiting some friends getting some drinks in Montclair and we saw/heard the makings of a punk show as we were walking past. We paid some weirdo a few bucks and went downstairs. It didn't look much different than it does now. It was a street punk band. Spikey hair, leather jackets, Doc Martens. Didn't pay much attention to it, just thought it was cool that was happening."[24]

He began to participate fully in 2005, after the closing of another local punk venue, the Bloomfield Ave Cafe. Peter captures the spirit of what it takes to keep a scene going:

> I remember that we didn't really even like it at first. There was no decent sound system (still isn't). The shows were sketchy (drugs, death metal kids that loved fighting everyone), but we had no other choice really. It was the only centrally located DIY space available and Roy rented it to us cheaper than what the halls could. Bathrooms break. If you work here you're going to clean up human shit. You're going to say to yourself, "Why the fuck do I do this for people that will kick a toilet until it cracks in half?" Someone's going to puke their heart out. If you don't clean it no one else is gunna.[25]

Occasional dustups with authorities and neighbors have shut the place down from time to time: "The Fire Marshall, well he doesn't like us and no one blames him. We stuff a bunch of kids into a box because if we don't those kids don't have anything else." Last year, a new tenant above the basement space did not appreciate the noise and annoyances that come with a musical venue, especially one that hosts punk shows. When the Locker was shut down, the kids flooded the new restaurant's Yelp page with one-star reviews and nasty (though often hilarious) critiques. There was a while when it seemed the Meatlocker might have come to its end. One local lamented, "Bands from all over the world have played here, it's crazy how many people know about the Locker outside of NJ and it has built up a great reputation over the years. Dan (Rivas) and Ana (Dobrian) have really cleaned it up and have worked hard to make it what it is today. It would be terrible to lose this place—for locals, touring bands, and the music and art community as a whole."[26] Another captured the spirit of the experience of the Meatlocker as "the base for a community where you can be yourself, lean on others for support, enjoy the best of times, and see really talented artists. It has been my haven for years now, and I am so thankful for that, but I'm also not okay with it ending. I know all good things must come to an end, but not this, at least not yet."[27]

Eventually, the responsible adults stepped in to do what they had to do to negotiate with all the neighbors, the landlord (who has been extremely supportive over the years), and local authorities. The Yelp reviews were removed, and the club reopened and outlasted the restaurant.

A dedicated group of organizers keep the place going, and new generations of teenagers continue discovering that unmatchable feeling of excitement mixed with terror that comes from descending the stairs into a space where anything can happen, and raucous, raw, and live music will be made. For the past several years a roving team of volunteers have paid the bills, booked the bands, dealt with sometimes unhappy neighbors and landlord. They stage benefit shows, including Mosh 4 Paws (after a fire at the local animal shelter), Lex Alex Nihilum's annual Sludge for Suicide Awareness, and Ana Dobrian's annual Toys for Tots event.

Peter, who still makes music, runs the sound board and books bands at various venues, and records other bands in a rickety studio above the garage of the house he rents on Orange Road. He remembers how formative the experience of the scene was in his life when his band Animal Blood played to racially diverse packed crowds with hip-hop bands from the small label associated with the local skate shop Division East:

> It's a giant part of who I am. It gave me purpose post going to war. It showed me the real meaning of giving. It's taught me how to just get it done. Murphy's Law is a bitch (not the band) and sometimes you have to just make whatever is in your way happen. You aren't going to get paid for it. No one's going to tell you good job, but at the end of the night you had a cool show and you were in the company of people that get you, even if you don't know them and what's better than that?[28]

The music business seems to be in continual crisis. Artists cannot make a living. Technology has replaced musicians. Streaming services pay an appallingly low amount to artists. Someone is making money, but it is not the musicians. But none of that really matters if you love music. Musicians and music lovers will continue making the scene in the Garden State because "all you really need is a bunch of kids that give a shit about where they are and what they are listening to."[29]

ACKNOWLEDGMENTS

This work would not exist without the initiative of Claudia Ocello, who came to me with the idea for the project some time ago. Although the original plan did not pan out, I am grateful for her support.

I never undertake any research without immediately consulting the inimitable Richard Kearney, the reference and electronic resource librarian at William Paterson University (WPU). His help has been invaluable, and it does not hurt that he knows as much about rock music and New Jersey as anyone. The whole staff at the Cheng Library at WPU has been indispensable, particularly the folks at Interlibrary Loan and the now-departed Victoria Heenan Wagner. I have received cheerful research assistance from Stephen Pellegrini, Bryan Payor, and Joel Cotton-Betteridge.

I could not have completed this project without a grant from the NJ350 Publication Initiative of the New Jersey Historical Commission. My thanks to its director, Sara R. Cureton, and to Skylar Harris for guiding me through the process. I was able to develop some of these ideas through presentations at the Morris Museum and the Mid-Atlantic Popular & American Culture Association.

At William Paterson University, Dean Kara Rabbitt and the Provost's office have supported me with research assistance. Meg Guenthner patiently assisted my passage through the funding labyrinth. I am deeply grateful to Malissa Williams for all her selfless support through the years.

At Rutgers University Press, I began this process under the able counsel of its director, Marlie P. Wasserman. Upon her retirement, I could not have been more fortunate than to have found Peter Mickulas, the executive editor. He edits with a light touch, but a firm understanding and clear vision. In the few times we have (mildly) disagreed, the work was strengthened by our discussion. At every step, working with Peter has been a joy and an inspiration.

A few of the chapters have exceptional photos. For these, I am grateful for help from Leonard DeGraaf, the archivist at Thomas Edison National Historical Park, and Valerie Sheffner, the museum technician; Angela Schad, a reference archivist and digital archives specialist at Hagley Museum and

Library; Mark Berresford at Mark Berresford Rare Records; Jim Testa at *Jersey Beat* for his generosity; and Michael Cuscuna, the director of Mosaic Records, who went to extraordinary lengths to help me with the stunning photos by Francis Wolff.

Perhaps more than most books, this one depends on the work of scholars and fans who have gone before me. I am especially indebted to the work of Allan Sutton and the extraordinary Mainspring Press; the interviews about Edison by John Harvith and Susan Edwards Harvith; Barry Mazor for his work on Ralph Peer and Jimmie Rodgers; Marc Myers of *JazzWax* for his numerous interviews with Rudy Van Gelder; Richard Scrivani for his magisterial memoir of Zacherley; Garry Wien for his history of music in Asbury Park; and especially Carrie Potter-Devening for her labor of love to her grandparents, the founders of the Upstage Club, a book filled with hundreds of photos and stories, which was truly indispensable in writing chapter 5.

I am ever grateful to those who trained me to be a historian, especially Berta Bilezikjian, D. Carroll Joynes, Carol Berkin, Stewart Ewen, and David Nasaw. Special thanks to Master Patricia Papera, Roger Sedarat, David Petroski, Kevin Delaney, Thee Volatiles, and all my friends in the Montclair music scene.

I dedicate this book to Sinéad and Rory, my children, because they are my two favorite people. I don't think I need any other reason than that.

Dewar MacLeod
January 2019

NOTES

INTRODUCTION

1. Richard A. Peterson and Andy Bennett, "Introducing Music Scenes," in Andy Bennett and A. Richard Peterson, *Music Scenes: Local, Translocal, and Virtual* (Nashville: Vanderbilt University Press, 2004), 1.

2. Peterson and Bennett, "Introducing Music Scenes," 3.

3. John Blacking quoted in Simon Frith, *Performing Rites: On the Value of Popular Music* (Cambridge, MA: Harvard University Press, 1996), 251.

4. For excellent reviews of the literature on subculture, post-subculture, and scenes, see Andy Bennett, "Consolidating the Music Scenes Perspective," *Poetics* 32, nos. 3–4 (2004): 223–234, and Andy Bennett, "The Post-subcultural Turn: Some Reflections 10 Years On," *Journal of Youth Studies* 14, no. 5 (August 2011): 493–506. For a useful survey of subcultural theory and post-subculture work (and a spirited defense of the Birmingham School [CCCS]), see Shane Blackman, "Youth Subcultural Theory: A Critical Engagement with the Concept, Its Origins and Politics, from the Chicago School to Postmodernism," *Journal of Youth Studies* 8, no. 1 (March 2005): 1–20.

5. Andy Bennett, "Subcultures or Neo-Tribes? Rethinking the Relationship between Youth, Style and Musical Taste," *Sociology* 33, no. 3 (August 1999): 599–617.

6. Rupert Weinzierl and David Muggleton, "What Is 'Post-subcultural Studies'?" in *The Post-Subcultures Reader*, edited by David Muggleton and Rupert Weinzierl, 3–4 (Oxford: Berg, 2003).

7. For an interesting perspective, see Dylan Clark on punk as "the last subculture," in "The Death and Life of Punk, The Last Subculture," in *Post-Subcultures Reader*, edited by Muggleton and Weinzierl, 223–238. See also Holly Kruse, "Subcultural Identity in Alternative Music Culture," *Popular Music* 12, no. 1 (1993): 33. Building on Sara Cohen's work on Liverpool musicians and Ruth Finnegan's study of Milton Keynes's musicians, Kruse links the local with the translocal, the national and international communities of music makers and listeners.

8. Benjamin Woo, Jamie Rennie, and Stuart R. Poyntz, "Scene Thinking," *Cultural Studies* 29, no. 3 (May 2015): 287, DOI: 10.1080/09502386.2014.937950.

9. Referencing Andy Bennett and Pepper Glass; Woo, Rennie, and Poyntz, "Scene Thinking," 287.

10. Woo, Rennie, and Poyntz, "Scene Thinking," 288. See Barry Shank, *Dissonant Identities: The Rock'n'Roll Scene in Austin, Texas* (Middletown, CT: Wesleyan University Press, 1994) and Will Straw, "Systems of Articulation, Logics of Change: Communities and Scenes in Popular Music," *Cultural Studies* 5 no. 3 (1991), 368–388, DOI: 10.1080/09502389100490311.

11. See Peterson and Bennett, "Introducing Music Scenes," 7.

12. Woo, Rennie, and Poyntz, "Scene Thinking," 288.

13. Citing Hesmondalgh's objections; Woo, Rennie, and Poyntz, "Scene Thinking," 291.

14. Will Straw, "Some Things a Scene Might Be," *Cultural Studies* 29, no. 3 (May 2015): 477, DOI: 10.1080/09502386.2014.937947.

15. The very flexibility of the concept of scene has provoked some criticism, leading one scholar to wonder if scene might be "a fruitfully muddled concept?" David Hesmondhalgh rejects subculture, scene, and Bennett's theorization of "neo-tribalism" as all too dependent on the examination of the relationship between young people and music. David Hesmondhalgh, "Subcultures, Scenes or Tribes? None of the Above," *Journal of Youth Studies* 8, no. 1 (March 2005): 27. Will Straw articulates the potentially too expansive and loose quality of the category of scene in "Scenes and Sensibilities," *Public* 22/23 (2001): 248. Summarizing Barry Shank's pioneering perspective in *Dissonant Identities*, Straw writes of the complexity and dense, sometimes impenetrable, meanings in "Cultural Scenes," *Loisir et société* [*Society and Leisure*] 27, no. 2 (2004): 412.

16. Thomas Turino, *Music as Social Life: The Politics of Participation* (Chicago: University of Chicago Press, 2008), 1.

17. Turino, *Music as Social Life*, 12.

18. Turino, *Music as Social Life*, 12.

19. "The fact that music matters so much to so many people may derive from two contrasting yet complementary dimensions of musical experience in modern societies. The first is that music often feels intensely and emotionally linked to the private self. As one writer has put it, music is a set of cultural practices that have come to be intricately bound up with the realm of the personal and the subjective. This includes the way in which music provides a basis for intimate relations with others: a parent singing a child to sleep; three sisters expressing their feelings for a fourth by singing to her on her birthday; two lovers in bed hearing a song that they will forever associate with each other. The second is that music is often the basis of collective, public experiences, whether in live performance, mad dancing at a party, or simply by virtue of the fact that thousands and sometimes millions of people can come to know the same sounds and performers." David Hesmondhalgh, *Why Music Matters* (Chichester, West Sussex, England: John Wiley, 2013), 1–2.

20. Simon Frith, "Towards an Aesthetic of Popular Music," in *Taking Popular Music Seriously: Selected Essays* (New York: Routledge, 2007), 261.

21. Frith, "Towards an Aesthetic of Popular Music," 265–66.

22. Frith, "Towards an Aesthetic of Popular Music," 266.

23. Frith, "Towards an Aesthetic of Popular Music," 267.

24. Mark Mattern, *Acting in Concert: Music, Community, and Political Action* (New Brunswick, NJ: Rutgers University Press, 1998), 4–5.

25. Samuel K. Byrd, *The Sounds of Latinidad: Immigrants Making Music and Creating Culture in a Southern City* (New York: New York University Press, 2015), 6.

26. Byrd, *Sounds of Latinidad*, 60–62.

27. Byrd, *Sounds of Latinidad*, 59.

28. Paul Hodkinson, "Translocal Connections in the Goth Scene," in Bennett and Peterson, *Music Scenes*, 144.

29. Hodkinson, "Translocal Connections in the Goth Scene," 146.

30. Howard S. Becker, "Jazz Places," in Bennett and Peterson, *Music Scenes*, 26.

31. Jeffrey S. Debies-Carl, *Punk Rock and the Politics of Place: Building a Better Tomorrow* (New York: Routledge, 2014), 7.

32. Travis A. Jackson, *Blowin' the Blues Away: Performance and Meaning on the New York Jazz Scene* (Berkeley: University of California Press, 2012), 67.

33. Charles Hersch, *Subversive Sounds: Race and the Birth of Jazz in New Orleans* (Chicago: University of Chicago Press, 2007), 24, 29, 37, 39.

34. Hersch, *Subversive Sounds*, 40.

35. Quoting Homi Bhabha; Hersch, *Subversive Sounds*, 41.

36. Hersch, *Subversive Sounds*, 47, 40. See also Andrew S. Berish, *Lonesome Roads and Streets of Dreams: Place, Mobility, and Race in Jazz of the 1930s and '40s* (Chicago: University of Chicago Press, 2012).

37. Christopher Small, *Musicking: The Meanings of Performing and Listening* (Middletown, CT: Wesleyan University Press, 2011), 9.

38. Thomas H. Greenland, *Jazzing: New York City's Unseen Scene* (Urbana: University of Illinois Press, 2016), 5–6.

39. Greenland, *Jazzing*, 7.

40. George Lewis quoted in Daniel Fischlein and Ajay Heble, eds., *The Other Side of Nowhere: Jazz, Improvisation, and Communities in Dialogue* (Middletown, CT: Wesleyan University Press, 2004), 3.

41. Fischlein and Heble, *Other Side of Nowhere*, 7.

42. Amy Absher, *The Black Musician and the White City: Race and Music in Chicago, 1900–1967* (Ann Arbor: University of Michigan Press, 2014), 7. See also the brilliant work by David Gilbert, *The Product of Our Souls: Ragtime, Race, and the Birth of the Manhattan Musical Marketplace* (Chapel Hill: University of North Carolina Press, 2015).

43. See Jason Toynbee, "Music, Culture, and Creativity," in *The Cultural Study of Music: A Critical Introduction*, edited by Martin Clayton, Trevor Herbert, and Richard Middleton, 102–103. (New York: Routledge, 2003).

44. Howard Becker quoted in Toynbee, "Music, Culture, and Creativity," 104. Toynbee also discusses Mikhail Bahktin's dialogism and Pierre Bourdieu's fields of cultural production.

45. Robert R. Faulkner, *Hollywood Studio Musicians: Their Work and Careers in the Recording Industry* (Lanham, MD: University Press of America, 1985; orig. 1971), 7–8.

46. Jonathan Gray, Cornel Sandvoss, and C. Lee Harrington, "Introduction: Why Study Fans?" in *Fandom: Identities and Communities in a Mediated World*, edited by Jonathan Gray, Cornel Sandvoss, and C. Lee Harrington, 2. (New York: New York University Press, 2007). See Michel de Certeau, *The Practice of Everyday Life* (Berkeley: University of California Press, 1984). See also Dewar MacLeod, *Kids of the Black Hole: Punk Rock in Postsuburban California* (Norman: University of Oklahoma Press, 2010).

47. Gray, Sandvoss, and Harrington, "Introduction," 6–9.

48. Gray, Sandvoss, and Harrington, "Introduction," 10.

49. Laura Vrooman, "Kate Bush: Teen Pop and Older Female Fans," in Bennett and Peterson, *Music Scenes*, 250.

50. Vrooman, "Kate Bush," 250–251.

51. Simon Frith, *Performing Rites: On the Value of Popular Music* (Cambridge, MA: Harvard University Press, 1996), 40–41, 20.

52. Frith, *Performing Rites*, 203–204.

53. Frith, *Performing Rites*, 205.

54. Frith, *Performing Rites*, 215.

55. Frith, *Performing Rites*, 252.

56. Frith, *Performing Rites*, 260. Frith describes music's "unique emotional intensity—we absorb songs into our own lives and rhythm into our own bodies," 272.

57. Frith, *Performing Rites*, 216, 272.

58. Frith, *Performing Rites*, 259.

59. Frith, *Performing Rites*, 272.

60. Frith, *Performing Rites*, 272, 275.

61. Frith, *Performing Rites*, 275.

62. Magdalena Waligórska-Huhle, "Introduction," in *Music, Longing and Belonging: Articulations of the Self and the Other in the Musical Realm*, edited by Magdalena Waligórska-Huhle, 1. (Newcastle upon Tyne: Cambridge Scholars, 2013).

63. Barry Shank, *The Political Force of Musical Beauty* (Durham, NC: Duke University Press, 2014), 1.

64. Shank, *Political Force of Musical Beauty*, 2.

65. Shank, *Political Force of Musical Beauty*, 2–3.

66. Shank, *Political Force of Musical Beauty*, 3.

67. Shank, *Political Force of Musical Beauty*, 244.

68. Shank, *Political Force of Musical Beauty*, 9.

69. Shank, *Political Force of Musical Beauty*, 245.

1. THOMAS EDISON AND THE FIRST RECORDING STUDIO

1. Edison quoted in W.K.L. Dickson and Antonia Dickson, *The Life and Inventions of Thomas Alva Edison* (London: Chatto and Windus, 1894), http://babel.hathitrust.org/cgi/pt?id=chi.57121461;view=1up;seq=11.

2. Roland Gelatt, *The Fabulous Phonograph*, 2nd rev. ed. (New York: Macmillan, 1976), 23.

3. Quoted in Russell Sanjek, *American Popular Music and Its Business, Volume II: From 1790 to 1909* (New York: Oxford University Press, 1988), 363.

4. Quoted in Andre Millard, *America on Record: A History of Recorded Sound* (New York: Cambridge University Press, 1995), 27.

5. Quoted in Frank Lewis Dyer and Thomas Commerford Martin, *Edison: His Life and Inventions* (orig. New York: Harper & Brothers Publishers, 1910), https://archive.org/details/edisonhislifeinvodyer.

6. Alexander Rehding, "Wax Cylinder Revolutions," *Musical Quarterly* 88, no. 1 (Spring 2005): 123.

7. David Suisman, *Selling Sounds: The Commercial Revolution in American Music* (Cambridge, MA: Harvard University Press, 2009), 5.

8. George H. Bliss, "Thomas A. Edison. A Tribune Correspondent Visits Him at Menlo Park: Some of His Recent Extraordinary Discoveries and Inventions," *Chicago Tribune*, May 4, 1878, http://www.phonozoic.net/n0060.htm.

9. "Etched": Emile Berliner, *The Gramophone: Etching the Human Voice* (Washington, DC: Judd and Detweiler, 1889). "Imprisoned": The musicologist Henry E. Krehbiel in 1891, quoted in Rehding, "Wax Cylinder Revolutions," 136, and Courtney Bryson quoted in Marsha Siefert, "Aesthetics, Technology, and the Capitalization of Culture: How the Talking Machine Became a Musical Instrument," *Science in Context* 8, no. 2 (1995): 419, DOI: 10.1017/S0269889700002088. "Preserved or bottled up...": George B. Prescott, "The Telephone and the Phonograph," *Scribner's Monthly* 15, no. 6 (April 1878): 848.
Emile Berliner, *The Gramophone: Etching the Human Voice* (Washington, DC: Judd and Detweiler, 1889).

10. Randall Stross, *The Wizard of Menlo Park: How Thomas Alva Edison Invented the Modern World* (New York: Crown, 2007), 34.

11. "Bottled Music," *Phonogram* 1, no. 1 (January 1891): 12.

12. Quoted in David Laing, "A Voice without a Face: Popular Music and the Phonograph in the 1890s," *Popular Music* 10, no. 1 (1991): 3–4.

13. Thomas Edison, "The Phonograph and Its Future," *North American Review* (July 1878): 530.

14. "The Man Who Invents: Tom Edison's Talk with a 'Post' Reporter," *Washington Post and Union*, April 19, 1878.

15. "Man Who Invents."

16. Alex Ross emphasizes Edison's claim to "annihilate time and space" that brought about a "global homogenization of taste." Alex Ross, *Listen to This* (New York: Farrar, Straus and Giroux, 2010), 57.

17. Quoted in Laing, "Voice without a Face," 3.

18. George Parsons Lathrop, "Talks with Edison," *Harper's New Monthly Magazine* 80, no. 477 (February 1890): 430.

19. "Man Who Invents."

20. See M. A. Rosanoff, "Edison in His Laboratory," *Harpers Monthly*, no. 165 (September 1932): 409.

21. Sanjek, *American Popular Music*, 364; "A Visit to the Inventor of the Phonograph," *Scientific American Supplement* (April 20, 1878): 1904–1905, http://www.phonozoic.net /n0014.htm; also published as *New York World* story reprinted in *Indiana State Sentinel*.

22. Rosanoff, "Edison in His Laboratory," 417.

23. "A Momentous Musical Meeting," *Etude* (October 1923): 663.

24. Lathrop, "Talks with Edison," 425.

25. Lathrop, "Talks with Edison," 429, 435.

26. See David E. Nye, *The Invented Self: An Anti-biography, from Documents of Thomas A. Edison* (Odense: Odense University Press, 1983), 102. Karen Halttunen, *Confidence Men and Painted Women: A Study of Middle-class Culture in America, 1830–1870* (New Haven, CT: Yale University Press, 1986).

27. *Times* (New Bloomfield, PA), April 30, 1878, Image 4, http://chroniclingamerica.loc
.gov/lccn/sn90069164/1878-04-30/ed-1/seq-4/.

28. Rosanoff, "Edison in His Laboratory," 404–406.

29. William H. Bishop, "A Night with Edison," *Scribner's Monthly* 17, no. 1 (November 1878): 98. Also: "He sits down at the phonograph, fixes a double mouth-piece to it and summons one of his assistants, while another places himself at an organ in the corner. They sing in two parts 'John Brown's Body.' As the sonorous music rises and fills the long apartment, one gazes musingly yet with a secret thrill. It is like assisting at some strange, new rite,—a martial chant of rejoicing in the greatness of a new era full of sublime promise and the dissipation of mysteries," 97.

30. "Edison in His Workshop," *Harper's Weekly* 23 (August 2, 1879): 607.

31. Bishop, "A Night with Edison," 88.

32. "Visit to the Inventor of the Phonograph."

33. Bliss, "Thomas A. Edison." See also Francis Jehl, *Menlo Park Reminiscences* (Dearborn, MI: Edison Institute, 1936).

34. PDF available at http://www.edisontinfoil.com/ephemer1.htm. Walter L. Welch, Leah Brodbeck Stenzel Burt, and Oliver Read, *From Tinfoil to Stereo: The Acoustic Years of the Recording Industry, 1877–1929* (Gainesville: University Press of Florida, 1995), 17.

35. Quoted in Sanjek, *American Popular Music*, 365.

36. Gelatt, *Fabulous Phonograph*, 30.

37. Sir W. H. Preece, quoted in Gelatt, *Fabulous Phonograph*, 31.

38. See Millard, *America on Record*, 32–34.

39. Welch, Burt, and Read, *From Tinfoil to Stereo*, 72. Raymond Wile, "Edison and Growing Hostilities," *ARSC Journal* 22, no. 1 (Spring 1991): 20.

40. Sanjek, *American Popular Music*, 367; Welch, Burt, and Read, *From Tinfoil to Stereo*, 87.

41. Welch, Burt, and Read, *From Tinfoil to Stereo*, 90.

42. Timothy Day, *A Century of Recorded Music: Listening to Musical History* (New Haven, CT: Yale University Press, 2000), 1. Day says Hofmann was eleven and the year was 1887. His footnotes seem more solid—since Gelatt has none! Gelatt, *Fabulous Phonograph*, 38. Gelatt says that in 1888, Hofmann, as a twelve-year-old piano prodigy, "visited the Edison laboratories to inspect the phonograph and engrave some cylinders."

43. "Facts, Rumours, and Remarks," *Musical Times and Singing Class Circular* 30, no. 558 (August 1, 1889): 468–473, http://www.jstor.org/stable/3360518. According to Roland Gelatt, "These were the first recordings to be made by any recognized artist. Not long after, the famous German musician Hans von Bülow came to examine the new apparatus. He recorded a Chopin mazurka, then put the tubes to ears and waited for the playback. What he heard caused him to faint dead away—though whether he was laid low by his own playing or merely by the poor reproduction of it has never been divulged" (Gelatt, *Fabulous Phonograph*, 39). Timothy Day says that Bülow "almost fainted," in *Century of Recorded Music*, 1.

44. Thomas A. Edison, "How Sound Is Reproduced," *Phonogram* 1, no. 1 (January 1891): 14.

45. Millard, *America on Record*, 44.

46. Lisa Gitelman, *Scripts, Grooves, and Writing Machines: Representing Technology in the Edison Era* (Stanford, CA: Stanford University Press, 1999), 171.

47. Susan Schmidt Horning, *Chasing Sound: Technology, Culture, and the Art of Studio Recording from Edison to the LP* (Baltimore: Johns Hopkins University Press, 2013), 13.

48. Horning, *Chasing Sound*, 14.

49. One historian claims that "very little recognition has been given to Thomas Edison and his able staff, including his son Theodore M. Edison, for their pioneering work in long playing recording. Many experiments done at the Columbia St. Studios were far ahead of their time in producing commercial recordings." Ronald Dethlefson, "Recordings of the Columbia St. Studios—West Orange," in Ronald Dethlefson, ed., *Edison Disc Artists & Records, 1919–1929*, 2nd ed. (Brooklyn: APM Press, 1990), 126.

50. Horning, *Chasing Sound*, 5.

51. Jerry Fabris, "WFMU-Thomas Edison's Attic: Playlist from April 19, 2005—Acoustical Recording Stories," http://wfmu.org/playlists/shows/14803.

52. Quoted in Day, *Century of Recorded Music*, 10.

53. In John Harvith and Susan Edwards Harvith, *Edison, Musicians, and the Phonograph: A Century in Retrospect* (New York: Greenwood Press, 1987), 43.

54. In Harvith and Harvith, *Edison, Musicians, and the Phonograph*, 80, 81.

55. Rosanoff, "Edison in His Laboratory," 403. See also Day, *Century of Recorded Music*, 10.

56. In Harvith and Harvith, *Edison, Musicians, and the Phonograph*, 111.

57. In Harvith and Harvith, *Edison, Musicians, and the Phonograph*, 65–66.

58. Day, *Century of Recorded Music*, 2.

59. Quoted in Horning, *Chasing Sound*, 14.

60. Fabris, "WFMU-Thomas Edison's Attic."

61. Quoted in Horning, *Chasing Sound*, 14.

62. Stevens in Harvith and Harvith, *Edison, Musicians, and the Phonograph*, 26–27. See also Bridget Paolucci, "Edison as Record Producer," *High Fidelity Magazine* (January 1977): 88.

63. Case quoted in Welch, Burt, and Read, *From Tinfoil to Stereo*, 146.

64. Emily Thompson, *The Soundscape of Modernity: Architectural Acoustics and the Culture of Listening in America, 1900–1933* (Cambridge, MA: MIT Press, 2004), 238.

65. Stevens in Harvith and Harvith, *Edison, Musicians, and the Phonograph*, 30.

66. Fabris, "WFMU-Thomas Edison's Attic."

67. See Stevens in Harvith and Harvith, *Edison, Musicians, and the Phonograph*, 26–27. See also Theodore M. Edison, "That horn, which was very large at one end and tapered down evenly to a normal receiving end, produced some interesting results, but I understand that for many purposes, an exponential horn could have achieved the same results in much smaller space." In Harvith and Harvith, *Edison, Musicians, and the Phonograph*, 40.

68. Dethlefson claims that Edison believed "that sound waves remained in an unfocused state for as much as 125′ beyond the source of a sound." See Dethlefson, "Recordings of the Columbia St. Studios," 126–127 for more on the 40- and 125-foot horns.

69. Victor Young, "Edison and Music," *Etude, the Music Magazine* (December 1932): 453.

70. Lathrop, "Talks with Edison," 426.

71. Stevens in Harvith and Harvith, *Edison, Musicians, and the Phonograph*, 26.

72. Young, "Edison and Music," 399.

73. Young, "Edison and Music," 453.

74. Edison quoted by Stevens in Harvith and Harvith, *Edison, Musicians, and the Phonograph*, 26.

75. Rosanoff, "Edison in His Laboratory," 413.

76. Stevens in Harvith and Harvith, *Edison, Musicians, and the Phonograph*, 29.

77. Stevens in Harvith and Harvith, *Edison, Musicians, and the Phonograph*, 31.

78. "Momentous Musical Meeting," 664.

79. Samuel Gardner in Harvith and Harvith, *Edison, Musicians, and the Phonograph*, 49.

80. Young, "Edison and Music," 399.

81. Gardner in Harvith and Harvith, *Edison, Musicians, and the Phonograph*, 48–49.

82. Gardner in Harvith and Harvith, *Edison, Musicians, and the Phonograph*, 49. Mark Katz has a brilliant analysis of the relationship between vibrato and the advent of recording. See "Aesthetics out of Exigency: Violin Vibrato and the Phonograph," in *Capturing Sound: How Technology Has Changed Music* (Berkeley: University of California Press, 2010), 94–108.

83. Young, "Edison and Music," 399.

84. Young, "Edison and Music," 399.

85. Stevens in Harvith and Harvith, *Edison, Musicians, and the Phonograph*, 25–26.

86. Stevens in Harvith and Harvith, *Edison, Musicians, and the Phonograph*, 32.

87. Edison Memorandum, May 11, 1912, Edison General File, Edison National Historic Site Archives, West Orange, New Jersey. Quoted in Leonard DeGraaf, "Confronting the Mass Market: Thomas Edison and the Entertainment Phonograph," *Business and Economic History* 24, no. 1 (Fall 1995): 93.

88. Young, "Edison and Music," 399.

89. Young, "Edison and Music," 399.

90. John Philip Sousa, "The Menace of Mechanical Music," *Appleton's Magazine* 8 (1906), 278–284, http://www.phonozoic.net/n0155.htm.

91. "Momentous Musical Meeting," 664.

92. DeGraaf, "Confronting the Mass Market," 94–95.

93. DeGraaf, "Confronting the Mass Market," 94–95.

94. Henry Ford and Samuel Crowther, *My Life and Work* (Garden City, NY: Doubleday, Page, 1923), 72.

95. Gitelman, *Scripts, Grooves, and Writing Machines*, 163.

96. DeGraaf, "Confronting the Mass Market," 95.

97. Letter circa 1916, quoted in Kathleen Mcauliffe, "The Undiscovered World of Thomas Edison," *Atlantic*, December 1, 1995, http://www.theatlantic.com/magazine/archive/1995/12/the-undiscovered-world-of-thomas-edison/305880/?single_page=true.

98. "Momentous Musical Meeting," 663.

99. Rosanoff, "Edison in His Laboratory," 415, 413.

100. "Momentous Musical Meeting," 664.

2. THE VICTOR TALKING MACHINE COMPANY
AND THE SCENE AT HOME

1. F. W. Gaisberg, *The Music Goes Round* (New York: Macmillan, 1942), 3–7.
2. See David Laing, "A Voice without a Face: Popular Music and the Phonograph in the 1890s," *Popular Music* 10, no. 1 (1991): 2.
3. Gaisberg, *Music Goes Round*, 6–7.
4. The classic formulations of the 1890s as a transitional period in American Culture are John Higham, "The Reorientation of American Culture in the 1890s" (orig. 1965), in *Hanging Together: Unity and Diversity in American Culture*, edited by John Higham and Carl Guarneri, 173–98 (New Haven, CT: Yale University Press, 2001), and Warren I. Susman, "'Personality' and the Making of Twentieth-Century Culture," in *Culture as History: The Transformation of American Society in the Twentieth Century* (New York: Pantheon Books, 1984), 271–86. A recent critique of Susman comes from Andrew R. Heinze, "Schizophrenia Americana: Aliens, Alienists and the 'Personality Shift' of Twentieth-Century Culture," *American Quarterly* 55, no. 2 (June 2003): 227–256. See also Rob Schorman, "The Truth about Good Goods: Clothing, Advertising, and the Representation of Cultural Values at the End of the Nineteenth Century," *American Studies* 37 (Spring 1996): 23–49.
5. Laing, "Voice without a Face," 6.
6. Laing, "Voice without a Face," 6.
7. Gaisberg, *Music Goes Round*, 8.
8. Gaisberg, *Music Goes Round*, 9–10.
9. Gaisberg, *Music Goes Round*, 12.
10. Gaisberg, *Music Goes Round*, 15.
11. George Reeser Prowell, *The History of Camden County, New Jersey* (Philadelphia: L. J. Richards, 1886), 532, http://www.ebooksread.com/authors-eng/george-reeser-prowell/the-history-of-camden-county-new-jersey-wor.shtml. For the carriage factory, see also http://www.coachbuilt.com/bui/c/collings/collings.htm. The official Victor history is B. L. Aldridge, *The Victor Talking Machine Company*, edited by Frederic Bayh (orig. Camden: RCA Sales Corporation,1964), http://www.davidsarnoff.org/vtm.html. For an in-depth account of Emile Berliner's invention of the gramophone, see Raymond R. Wile, "Etching the Human Voice: The Berliner Invention of the Gramophone," *ARSC Journal* 21, no. 1 (1990): 2–22.
12. Johnson quoted in Jerrold Northrop Moore, *Sound Revolutions: A Biography of Fred Gaisberg, Founding Father of Commercial Sound Recording* (London: Sanctuary, 1999), 27.
13. According to Aldridge, in *Victor Talking Machine Company*, commercially, the Berliner process had five important advantages:

1. A record groove which formed track to guide the sound box across the record. (No propelling mechanism was needed.)
2. Grooves with hard walls which provided support for the needle and resulted in louder reproduction and protection against wear.
3. Ease and economy in making a large number of duplicate records.

4. Better musical results from the lateral process of recording.

5. Ease and economy in shipment and storage.

14. Quoted in Lisa Gitelman, *Scripts, Grooves, and Writing Machines: Representing Technology in the Edison Era* (Stanford, CA: Stanford University Press, 1999), 157.

15. David Suisman, *Selling Sounds: The Commercial Revolution in American Music* (Cambridge, MA: Harvard University Press, 2009), 5–6.

16. Laing, "Voice without a Face," 2.

17. Suisman, *Selling Sounds*, 9.

18. Suisman, *Selling Sounds*, 10, 12.

19. Wile, "Etching the Human Voice," 2–22.

20. See Barry Ashpole, "A Conversation with John Bolig," *ARSC Journal*, reprinted with permission from *ARSC Journal* (Spring 2003), http://www.mainspringpress.com/caruso_interview.html.

21. Ashpole, "Conversation with John Bolig."

22. Quoted in Howard S. Greenfield, *Caruso, An Illustrated Life* (North Pomfret, VT: Trafalgar Square, 1991), 33.

23. Quoted in Greenfield, *Caruso*, 42.

24. Melba quoted in Greenfield, *Caruso*, 49.

25. Enrico Caruso Jr. and Andrew Farkas, *Enrico Caruso: My Father and My Family* (Portland, OR: Amadeus Press, 1990), 349. Alex Ross notes, "That ping in Caruso's tone, that golden bark, made the man himself seem viscerally present." Alex Ross, *Listen to This* (New York: Farrar, Straus and Giroux, 2010), 57.

26. Greenfield, *Caruso*, 47. There is some doubt as to the truth of this often-told story. Moore contends that Gaisberg was able to ignore the cable forbidding him to sign Caruso because he had already decided to pay it out of his own pocket. Moore, *Sound Revolutions*, 69.

27. Gaisberg quoted in Greenfield, *Caruso*, 48.

28. Roland Gelatt, *The Fabulous Phonograph*, 2nd rev. ed. (New York: Macmillan, 1976), 115.

29. Marsha Siefert, "The Audience at Home: The Early Recording Industry and the Marketing of Musical Taste," in *Audiencemaking: How the Media Create the Audience*, edited by James S. Ettema and D. Charles Whitney, 195 (Thousand Oaks, CA: Sage, 1994).

30. Caruso and Farkas, *Enrico Caruso*, 346.

31. Quoted in Greenfield, *Caruso*, 132.

32. Edward L. Bernays, *Biography of an Idea: The Founding Principles of Public Relations* (New York: Open Road Integrated Media, 2015; orig. 1965), http://books.google.com/books?id=tFO2BgAAQBAJ&q=caruso#v=onepage&q&f=false.

33. See Greenfield, *Caruso*, 68, 71.

34. Bernays, *Biography of an Idea*.

35. Compton Mackenzie, Foreword to J. Freestone and H. J. Drummond, *Enrico Caruso: His Recorded Legacy* (Minneapolis: T. S. Denison, 1961), ix.

36. Caruso and Farkas, *Enrico Caruso*, 286–287.

37. Caruso and Farkas, *Enrico Caruso*, 363.

38. William R. Moran, "Discography of Original Recordings," in Caruso and Farkas, *Enrico Caruso*, 603–604.

39. Compton Mackenzie, "Enrico Caruso," *Gramophone* (July 1924): 45.

40. Mackenzie, "Enrico Caruso," 45.

41. On high/low, see the classic by Lawrence W. Levine, *Highbrow / Lowbrow: The Emergence of Cultural Hierarchy in America* (Cambridge, MA: Harvard University Press, 1999).

42. Siefert, "Audience at Home," 187.

43. Siefert, "Audience at Home," 195.

44. Barzun quoted in Michael Chanan, *Repeated Takes: A Short History of Recording and Its Effects on Music* (New York: Verso, 1995), 12.

45. *Talking Machine World* 1, no. 10 (October 15, 1905), https://archive.org/stream/The TalkingMachineWord1905Volume1/TheTalkingMachineWorld1905#page/n275/mode /2up.

46. Eisenberg, quoted in David Laing, "Voice without a Face," 8.

47. See Siefert, "Audience at Home," 209.

48. Marie Sumner Lott, *The Social Worlds of Nineteenth-Century Chamber Music: Composers, Consumers, Communities* (Champaign: University of Illinois Press, 2015), 4.

49. Lott, *Social Worlds*, 18.

50. Lott, *Social Worlds*, 20.

51. Daniel Cavicchi, "Loving Music: Listeners, Entertainments, and the Origins of Music Fandom in Nineteenth-Century America," in *Fandom: Identities and Communities in a Mediated World*, edited by Jonathan Gray, Cornel Sandvoss, and C. Lee Harrington, 236 (New York: New York University Press, 2007).

52. Cavicchi, "Loving Music," 239.

53. Cavicchi, "Loving Music," 246.

54. Pamela Robertson Wojcik, "The Girl and the Phonograph; or, The Vamp and the Machine Revisited," in *Soundtrack Available: Essays on Film and Popular Music*, edited by Arthur Knight and Pamela Robertson Wojcik (Durham, NC: Duke University Press, 2001). Pamela Robertson Wojcik notes how women and girls are depicted in advertising and popular culture, especially film, as gaining access to auditory power through the phonograph, and using the technology for "private, even solo, pleasure." 452. See also Nathan David Bowers, "Creating a Home Culture for the Phonograph: Women and the Rise of Sound Recordings in the United States, 1877–1913," (PhD diss., University of Pittsburgh, 2007 (UMI Number: 3270123)).

55. Wojcik, "Girl and the Phonograph," 435. See also Holly Kruse, "Early Audio Technology and Domestic Space," *Stanford Humanities Review* 3, no. 2 (1993): 1–14.

56. Kruse, "Early Audio Technology," 1.

57. Kruse, "Early Audio Technology," 8.

58. See also Susan C. Cook, "Talking Machines, Dancing Bodies: Marketing Recorded Dance Music before World War I," in *Bodies of Sound: Studies across Popular Music and Dance*, edited by Sherril Dodds and Susan C. Cook, 153 (New York: Routledge, 2016).

59. The ratio of popular to Red Seal was close to five-to-one in the teens and twenties. See "Victor Record Sales Statistics (1901–1941)," http://www.mainspringpress.com/victorsales.html.

60. See Tim Brooks, *Lost Sounds: Blacks and the Birth of the Recording Industry, 1890–1919* (Urbana: University of Illinois Press, 2004); Tim Brooks, "'Might Take One Disc of This Trash as a Novelty': Early Recordings by the Fisk Jubilee Singers and the Popularization of 'Negro Folk Music,'" *American Music* 18, no. 3 (Autumn 2000): 283; Paul Robeson Jr., *The Undiscovered Paul Robeson: An Artists Journey, 1898–1939* (New York: John Wiley, 2001), 93.

61. See Nathaniel Shilkret, *Sixty Years in the Music Business* (Lanham, MD: Scarecrow Press, 2005).

62. Allan Sutton, "Camden, Philadelphia, or New York? The Victor Studio Conundrum (1900–20)," http://www.mainspringpress.com/vic-studios.html.

63. From *A New Graded List of Victor Records for the Home, Kindergarten and School*, Education Department, Victor Talking Machine Company, 1918. Available as "Victor Discography: How Recordings Are Made in the Victor Laboratory," http://victor.library.ucsb.edu/index.php/resources/detail/54.

64. The daily whistles were finally halted in 1923. See Allan Sutton, "A Camden Chronology: The Evolution of the Victor Talking Machine Company Complex (1899–1929)," http://www.mainspringpress.com/vic-camden.html.

65. "Victor Co. Announces Plans for Radiola Installation in Victor Talking Machines," *Talking Machine World*, New York, June 15, 1925, http://www.sfmuseum.org/hist2/radiola.html. See also Aldridge, *Victor Talking Machine Company*.

66. Barry Mazor, *Ralph Peer and the Making of Popular Roots Music* (Chicago: Chicago Review Press, 2015), 11–21.

67. For Peer's role in the production and distribution of the record, see Mazor, *Ralph Peer*, 37–43.

68. Mazor, *Ralph Peer*, 76–77.

69. Ralph Peer, 1955 letter to folklorist John Greenway, quoted in Mazor, *Ralph Peer*, 1. For multiple fascinating perspectives on Jimmie Rodgers, see Mary Davis and Warren Zanes, eds., *Waiting for a Train: Jimmie Rodgers's America* (Burlington, MA: Rounder Books, 2009).

70. Jessica H. Foy, "The Home Set to Music," in *The Arts and the American Home, 1890–1930*, edited by Jessica H. Foy and Karal Ann Marling, 62–84 (Knoxville: University of Tennessee Press, 1994).

3. JAZZ AT THE CLIFFSIDE

1. Scott DeVeaux, *The Birth of Bebop: A Social and Musical History* (Berkeley: University of California Press, 1997), 29.

2. DeVeaux, *Birth of Bebop*, 30.

3. See Jason Toynbee, "Music, Culture, and Creativity," in *The Cultural Study of Music: A Critical Introduction*, edited by Martin Clayton, Trevor Herbert, and Richard Middleton, 102–103 (New York: Routledge, 2003).

4. Howard Becker, quoted in Toynbee, "Music, Culture, and Creativity," 104. Toynbee also discusses Mikhail Bakhtin's dialogism and Pierre Bourdieu's fields of cultural production.

5. DeVeaux, *Birth of Bebop*, 204.

6. DeVeaux, *Birth of Bebop*, 30, 171.

7. DeVeaux, *Birth of Bebop*, 217.

8. DeVeaux, *Birth of Bebop*, 212.

9. DeVeaux, *Birth of Bebop*, 203.

10. DeVeaux, *Birth of Bebop*, 210.

11. DeVeaux, *Birth of Bebop*, 214.

12. DeVeaux, *Birth of Bebop*, 220.

13. "RIP Rudy Van Gelder (1924–2016)," BlueNote.com, August 25, 2016, http://www
.bluenote.com/news/rip-rudy-van-gelder. Vicki Hyman, "N.J. Jazz Giant Rudy Van
Gelder, Who Recorded John Coltrane, Miles Davis, Dead at 91," NJ.com, August 25, 2016,
http://www.nj.com/entertainment/celebrities/index.ssf/2016/08/rudy_van_gelder
_jazz_recording_engineer_obituary.html.

14. Van Gelder quoted in Marc Myers, "Rudy Van Gelder (1924–2016)," *JazzWax*,
August 26, 2016 (from article originally in *Wall Street Journal*, February 7, 2012), http://
www.jazzwax.com/2016/08/rudy-van-gelder-1924-2016.html.

15. Marc Myers, "Interview: Rudy Van Gelder (Part 2)," *JazzWax*, February 14, 2012,
http://www.jazzwax.com/2012/02/interview-rudy-van-gelder-part-2.html.

16. A key source is Myers, "Rudy Van Gelder (1924–2016)."

17. Associated Press, "Rudy Van Gelder, Engineer behind Sound of Modern Jazz, Dies
Aged 91," *The Guardian*, August 28, 2016, https://www.theguardian.com/music/2016/aug
/28/rudy-van-gelder-blue-note-records-dead.

18. Van Gelder quoted in "Rudy Van Gelder, Great Jazz Recording Engineer—Obituary,"
Telegraph, September 2, 2016, http://www.telegraph.co.uk/obituaries/2016/09/02/rudy
-van-gelder-great-jazz-recording-engineer—obituary/.

19. Rudy Van Gelder, NEA interviews, at "National Endowment for the Arts Statement
on the Death of NEA Jazz Master Rudy Van Gelder," August 26, 2016, https://www.arts
.gov/news/2016/national-endowment-arts-statement-death-nea-jazz-master-rudy-van
-gelder. See also Kyle Kelly-Yahner, "Miles Davis, Rudy Van Gelder, and a Living Room
Recording Studio (Part 2 of 2)," *National Museum of American History Blog*, September 15,
2011, http://americanhistory.si.edu/blog/2011/09/miles-davis-rudy-van-gelder-and-a
-living-room-recording-studio-part-2-of-2-.html.

20. Eric D. Daniel, C. Denis Mee, and Mark H. Clark, eds., *Magnetic Recording: The First
100 Years* (New York: IEEE Press, 1999). Steven Schoenherr, "The History of Magnetic
Recording," November 5, 2002, http://www.aes.org/aeshc/docs/recording.technology
.history/magnetic4.html.

21. Sasha Zand, "Interview: Rudy Van Gelder: Recording Coltrane, Miles, Monk, etc.,"
Tape Op, no. 43 (September/October 2004), http://tapeop.com/interviews/43/rudy
-van-gelder/.

22. Marc Myers, "Interview: Rudy Van Gelder (Part 1)," *JazzWax*, February 13, 2012,
http://www.jazzwax.com/2012/02/interview-rudy-van-gelder-part-1.html.

23. Marc Myers, "Interview: Rudy Van Gelder (Part 4)," *JazzWax*, February 16, 2012, http://www.jazzwax.com/2012/02/interview-rudy-van-gelder-part-4.html.

24. Myers, "Interview: Rudy Van Gelder (Part 1)."

25. Not white gloves, as was often claimed, but "plain brown cotton work gloves." See Myers, "Interview: Rudy Van Gelder (Part 4)."

26. Myers, "Interview: Rudy Van Gelder (Part 1)."

27. Myers, "Interview: Rudy Van Gelder (Part 1)."

28. Myers, "Interview: Rudy Van Gelder (Part 3)," *JazzWax*, February 15, 2012, http://www.jazzwax.com/2012/02/interview-rudy-van-gelder-part-3.html.

29. Myers, "Interview: Rudy Van Gelder (Part 3)."

30. Myers, "Interview: Rudy Van Gelder (Part 3)."

31. Myers, "Interview: Rudy Van Gelder (Part 3)."

32. Dan Skea, "Rudy Van Gelder in Hackensack: Defining the Jazz Sound in the 1950s," *Current Musicology*, nos. 71–73 (Spring 2001–2002): 64.

33. Myers, "Interview: Rudy Van Gelder (Part 3)."

34. Myers, "Interview: Rudy Van Gelder (Part 3)."

35. Ira Gitler, "Vangelder's Studio," *JazzTimes*, April 2001, http://jazztimes.com/articles/20326-vangelder-s-studio.

36. Van Gelder quoted in Daniel Kreps, "Rudy Van Gelder, Renowned 'A Love Supreme' Engineer, Dead at 91," *Rolling Stone*, August 26, 2016, http://www.rollingstone.com/music/news/rudy-van-gelder-a-love-supreme-engineer-dead-at-92-w436307.

37. Myers, "Interview: Rudy Van Gelder (Part 3)."

38. Van Gelder quoted in Myers, "Rudy Van Gelder (1924–2016)."

39. Gitler, "Vangelder's Studio."

40. Associated Press, "Rudy Van Gelder."

41. Skea, "Rudy Van Gelder in Hackensack," 68.

42. Van Gelder quoted in Myers, "Rudy Van Gelder (1924–2016)."

43. Myers, "Rudy Van Gelder (1924–2016)."

44. Myers, "Rudy Van Gelder (1924–2016)."

45. Myers, "Rudy Van Gelder (1924–2016)."

46. Myers, "Rudy Van Gelder (1924–2016)."

47. Richard Brody, "Postscript: Rudy Van Gelder (1924–2016), Modern Jazz's Listener of Genius," *New Yorker*, August 26, 2016, http://www.newyorker.com/culture/richard-brody/postscript-rudy-van-gelder-1924-2016-modern-jazzs-listener-of-genius.

48. Myers, "Interview: Rudy Van Gelder (Part 4)."

49. Nate Chinen, "How Rudy Van Gelder Shaped the Sound of Jazz as We Know It," *New York Times*, August 26, 2016, http://www.nytimes.com/2016/08/27/arts/music/rudy-van-gelder-essential-recordings.html?_r=0.

50. Brody, "Postscript."

51. Brody, "Postscript."

52. Billy Taylor quoted in Skea, "Rudy Van Gelder in Hackensack," 59–60.

53. Marc Myers, "ARENA—Music—Anatomy of a Song: Deacon Blues: 'They Call Alabama The Crimson Tide,'" *Wall Street Journal*, September 11, 2015: D.1.

54. Van Gelder quoted in Kreps, "Rudy Van Gelder."
55. Skea, "Rudy Van Gelder in Hackensack," 60.
56. Michael Cuscuna, interview by Dean Schaffer, "Secrets of the Blue Note Vault," *Collectors Weekly*, August 20, 2010, http://www.collectorsweekly.com/articles/secrets-of-the-blue-note-vault-michael-cuscuna-on-monk-blakey-and-the-one-that-got-away/.
57. Jim Cogan and William Clark, *Temples of Sound: Inside the Great Recording Studios* (San Francisco: Chronicle Books, 2003), 194.
58. Alfred Lion quoted in Skea, "Rudy Van Gelder in Hackensack," 69.
59. Alfred Lion quoted in Ted Fox, *In the Groove: The People Behind the Music* (New York: St. Martin's Press, 1986), 111.
60. Rudy van Gelder quoted in Skea, "Rudy Van Gelder in Hackensack," 69.
61. Rudy Van Gelder quoted in Cogan and Clark, *Temples of Sound*, 196.
62. Alfred Lion quoted in Cogan and Clark, *Temples of Sound*, 199.
63. Rudy Van Gelder, interview in Ben Sidran, *Talking Jazz: An Oral History*, exp. ed. (Boston: Da Capo Press, 1995), 314.
64. Bob Weinstock quoted in Cogan and Clark, *Temples of Sound*, 198.
65. Martin Gayford, "Blue Note Records: From Ammons to Monk, It Was Home to the Jazz Idealists," *Telegraph*, July 15, 2009, https://www.telegraph.co.uk/culture/music/worldfolkandjazz/5777401/Blue-Note-Records-from-Ammons-to-Monk-it-was-home-to-the-jazz-idealists.html.
66. "James Rozzi Interview with Rudy Van Gelder," *Audio Magazine*, November 1995, reprinted in Steven Cerra, "Rudy van Gelder: A Signature Sound," *Jazz Profiles*, May 8, 2011, https://jazzprofiles.blogspot.com/2011/05/rudy-van-gelder-signature-sound.html.
67. "James Rozzi Interview with Rudy Van Gelder."
68. Chinen, "How Rudy Van Gelder Shaped the Sound."
69. Skea, "Rudy Van Gelder in Hackensack," 72.
70. Van Gelder quoted in Skea, "Rudy Van Gelder in Hackensack," 72.
71. Johnny Griffin quoted in Alyn Shipton, *A New History of Jazz*, rev. and updated ed. (New York: Continuum, 2007), 492–493.
72. Ashley Kahn, *A Love Supreme: The Story of John Coltrane's Signature Album* (New York: Penguin Books, 2002), 90.
73. Van Gelder, NEA interviews.
74. Cary Thomas, *Bebop: The Music and Its Players* (New York: Oxford University Press, 1996), 117.
75. Michael Cuscana quoted in Thomas Staudter, "Trane Tracks," *Downbeat* (September 2014): 32.
76. Skea, "Rudy Van Gelder in Hackensack," 62.
77. George Hicks, "Rudy Van Gelder Heard the Sound of the Future in the Music of His Time," *ARTery*, September 1, 2016, http://www.wbur.org/artery/2016/09/01/rudy-van-gelder.
78. Burt Korall, *Drummin' Men: The Heartbeat of Jazz, The Swing Years* (Cary, NC: Oxford University Press, 2004), 84–85. ProQuest ebrary.
79. Thomas, *Bebop*, 182.

80. Robin D. G. Kelley, *Thelonious Monk: The Life and Times of an American Original* (New York: Free Press, 2009), 183.

81. Ira Gitler, liner notes to *Miles Davis and the Modern Jazz Giants*, Prestige LP 7150.

82. André Hodier quoted in Peter Losin, "Miles Ahead Session Details," *Miles Ahead: A Miles Davis Website*, http://www.plosin.com/MilesAhead/Sessions.aspx?s=541224.

83. Losin, "Miles Ahead Session Details."

84. Zand, "Interview: Rudy Van Gelder."

85. Zand, "Interview: Rudy Van Gelder."

86. Davis quoted in Tom Reney, "Miles Davis All Stars: At Work On Christmas Eve," New England Pubic Radio, December 24, 2014, http://digital.nepr.net/music/2014/12/24/miles-davis-all-stars/.

87. Rudy Van Gelder quoted in Cogan and Clark, *Temples of Sound*, 199.

88. Miles Davis and Quincy Troupe, *Miles, the Autobiography.* (New York: Simon and Schuster, 1990), 80.

89. Davis quoted in Reney, "Miles Davis All Stars."

90. Thelonious Monk quoted in Kelley, *Thelonious Monk*, 182.

91. Bob Weinstock quoted in *The Prestige Records Story* [sound recording]. Berkeley: Prestige, 1999.

92. Zand, "Interview: Rudy Van Gelder."

93. Gitler, liner notes to *Miles Davis and the Modern Jazz Giants*.

94. Monk quoted in Kelley, *Thelonious Monk*, 184.

95. Reney, "Miles Davis All Stars."

96. Marc Myers, "Interview: Rudy Van Gelder (Part 5)," *JazzWax*, February 17, 2012, http://www.jazzwax.com/2012/02/interview-rudy-van-gelder-part-5.html.

97. Myers, "Rudy Van Gelder (1924–2016)."

98. Van Gelder quoted in Myers, "Rudy Van Gelder (1924–2016)."

99. Marc Myers, "Interview: Rudy Van Gelder (Part 5)."

100. Van Gelder, NEA interviews.

101. Myers, "Rudy Van Gelder (1924–2016)."

102. Myers, "Rudy Van Gelder (1924–2016)."

103. Kahn, *Love Supreme*, 89.

104. Producer Phil Ramone, quoted in Kahn, *Love Supreme*, 91.

105. Skea, "Rudy Van Gelder in Hackensack," 54.

106. Lewis MacAdams, *Birth of the Cool: Beat, Bebop, and the American Avant-Garde* (New York: Free Press, 2001), 63.

107. Skea, "Rudy Van Gelder in Hackensack," 54.

108. Skea, "Rudy Van Gelder in Hackensack," 54.

109. Skea, "Rudy Van Gelder in Hackensack," 54.

110. Van Gelder quoted in Myers, "Rudy Van Gelder (1924–2016)."

111. Zand, "Interview: Rudy Van Gelder."

112. Myers, "Interview: Rudy Van Gelder (Part 5)."

113. Van Gelder quoted in Myers, "Rudy Van Gelder (1924–2016)."

114. Mingus quoted in Leonard Feather, "Blindfold Test: Charlie Mingus," *Downbeat Magazine*, April 28, 1960; reprint, http://mingusmingusmingus.com/mingus/blindfold-test.
115. Myers, "Interview: Rudy Van Gelder (Part 5)."
116. Van Gelder, NEA interviews.

4. TRANSYLVANIA BANDSTAND AND ROCKIN'
WITH THE COOL GHOUL

1. "The Cool Ghoul"—"an appellation bestowed upon him by Dick Clark following the release of 'Dinner With Drac' in 1958." Richard Scrivani, *"Good Night, Whatever You Are!" My Journey with Zacherley, the Cool Ghoul* (New York: Dinoship, 2006), 66.
2. Ad reprinted in Scrivani, *"Good Night, Whatever You Are!"* 51.
3. David Colton, Preface to Scrivani, *"Good Night, Whatever You Are!"* 3.
4. Quoted in Scrivani, *"Good Night, Whatever You Are!"* 50.
5. David Colton, Preface to Scrivani, *"Good Night, Whatever You Are!"* 2.
6. Yahoo *Disc-O-Teen* Discussion Group, no. 587 (archive in the author's possession.)
7. See Scrivani, *"Good Night, Whatever You Are!"* 95.
8. Scrivani, *"Good Night, Whatever You Are!"* 80.
9. Scrivani, *"Good Night, Whatever You Are!"* 78.
10. "*Community* represents a theoretical and practical means through which disparate individuals come to recognize and act upon common concerns and interests, negotiate differences, and assert themselves in public arenas." Mark Mattern, *Acting in Concert: Music, Community, and Political Action* (New Brunswick, NJ: Rutgers University Press, 1998), 4–5.
11. For another example that theorizes issues of identity and community, see Samuel K. Byrd, *The Sounds of Latinidad: Immigrants Making Music and Creating Culture in a Southern City* (New York: New York University Press, 2015), 5, 59–62.
12. For another example from a different era, see Paul Hodkinson, "Translocal Connections in the Goth Scene," in *Music Scenes: Local, Translocal, and Virtual*, edited by Andy Bennett and A. Richard Peterson, 144–146 (Nashville, TN: Vanderbilt University Press, 2004).
13. See Joe Austin and Michael Nevin Willard, eds., *Generations of Youth: Youth Cultures and History in Twentieth-Century America* (New York: New York University Press, 1998) and Tracey Skelton and Gill Valentine, eds., *Cool Places: Geographies of Youth Cultures* (New York: Routledge, 1998). See also Doreen Massey, "The Spatial Construction of Youth Cultures," in Skelton and Valentine, *Cool Places*, 123–126.
14. Ben Malbon, "Clubbing: Consumption, Identity and the Spatial Practices of Every-Night Life," in *Cool Places*, edited by Skelton and Valentine, 280.
15. Colin Helb, "'The Time Is Right to Set Our Sight on Salvation': The Strange Tale of How the Hare Krishnas Came to Play Hardcore Punk," in *Hardcore, Punk, and Other Junk: Aggressive Sounds in Contemporary Music*, edited by Eric James Abbey and Colin Helb, 162 (Lanham, MD: Lexington Books, 2014). See also Steven Blush's oral history, *American Hardcore: A Tribal History* (Port Townsend, WA: Feral House, 2001).

16. Thomas Turino, *Music as Social Life: The Politics of Participation* (Chicago: University of Chicago Press, 2008), 26, 35.

17. Nick Crossley, *Networks of Sound, Style and Subversion: The Punk and Post-Punk Worlds of Manchester, London, Liverpool and Sheffield, 1975–1980* (Manchester: Manchester University Press, 2015), 4, 9–10.

18. Crossley, *Networks of Sound*, 80, 35.

19. Yahoo *Disc-O-Teen* Discussion Group, no. 317.

20. Yahoo *Disc-O-Teen* Discussion Group, nos. 265, 1273, and 1276.

21. Nancy Semon-Krauss in "Remembering When," *Newark Star-Ledger*, November 1, 2007.

22. Diane W., Yahoo *Disc-O-Teen* Discussion Group, no. 654.

23. See Yahoo *Disc-O-Teen* Discussion Group, no. 705.

24. Yahoo *Disc-O-Teen* Discussion Group, no. 368.

25. Yahoo *Disc-O-Teen* Discussion Group, no. 261.

26. Yahoo *Disc-O-Teen* Discussion Group, no. 74.

27. Yahoo *Disc-O-Teen* Discussion Group, no. 1114.

28. Yahoo *Disc-O-Teen* Discussion Group, nos. 265, 302, and 291.

29. Yahoo *Disc-O-Teen* Discussion Group, nos. 300 and 302,

30. John T., Yahoo *Disc-O-Teen* Discussion Group, no. 318.

31. Yahoo *Disc-O-Teen* Discussion Group, nos. 532, 533, 534, 535, and 536.

32. Yahoo *Disc-O-Teen* Discussion Group, nos. 265, 26, and 274.

33. Yahoo *Disc-O-Teen* Discussion Group, no. 38.

34. Yahoo *Disc-O-Teen* Discussion Group, no. 296.

35. Yahoo *Disc-O-Teen* Discussion Group, no. 626.

36. For other excellent studies of girl cultures, see Melanie Lowe, "'Tween' Scene: Resistance within the Mainstream," and Kristen Schilt, "'Riot Grrrl Is . . .': The Contestation over Meaning in a Music Scene," in Bennett and Peterson, *Music Scenes*.

37. Yahoo *Disc-O-Teen* Discussion Group, no. 123.

38. Yahoo *Disc-O-Teen* Discussion Group, numerous.

39. Richard X. Heyman, *Boom Harangue* (Bloomington, IN: iUniverse, 2002).

40. Interview with Brian Lippey, December 23, 2010. See also Yahoo *Disc-O-Teen* Discussion Group, nos. 863, 1488, and 1538 for more club listings.

41. http://60sgaragebands.com/1910fruitgumcompany.html.

42. Scrivani, *"Good Night, Whatever You Are!"* 162.

43. Themes included Beach (January 21, 196?), Scrivani, *"Good Night, Whatever You Are!"* 106; Hillbilly, date unknown, Scrivani, *"Good Night, Whatever You Are!"* 109; Vampire's Ball, February 18, 1966, Scrivani, *"Good Night, Whatever You Are!"* 109; Roman, March 1966, Scrivani, *"Good Night, Whatever You Are!"* 115; Spy Show, taped Friday March 25, 1966, Scrivani, *"Good Night, Whatever You Are!"* 117; and Dinosaur Egg Roll, April 8, 1966 (?), Scrivani, *"Good Night, Whatever You Are!"* 130.

44. Scrivani, *"Good Night, Whatever You Are!"* 90. Yahoo *Disc-O-Teen* Discussion Group, nos. 284 and 299.

45. Show appears to have been June 15, 1967 (see Yahoo *Disc-O-Teen* Discussion Group, no. 679), though some remember July 1967. It appears that "Light My Fire" hit no. 1 on July 29, 1967, and stayed there for three weeks; see http://www.billboard.com/specials/hot100/charts/weekly-no1s-60s.shtml; and http://en.wikipedia.org/wiki/List_of_Billboard_Hot_100_number-one_singles_of_1967. Landers remembers the show as "their first appearance on television" though this is doubtful (Yahoo *Disc-O-Teen* Discussion Group, no. 1293). Landers and members of the Gilgos 5 (who claim to have appeared, and remember it as Beach Bum Party day) remember the Doors lip-synching (Yahoo *Disc-O-Teen* Discussion Group, nos. 633, 679, and 1293). Chips & Co. also claims to have appeared (Yahoo *Disc-O-Teen* Discussion Group, no. 1286).

46. Joe LoRe', Yahoo *Disc-O-Teen* Discussion Group, no. 9.

47. Landers, Yahoo *Disc-O-Teen* Discussion Group, no. 1293. See also Yahoo *Disc-O-Teen* Discussion Group, nos. 679 and 1286.

48. David Dutkowski, "personal communication to author," July 23, 2019. Yahoo *Disc-O-Teen* Discussion Group, no. 266.

49. Yahoo *Disc-O-Teen* Discussion Group, no. 679.

50. Dave at http://manzarek.thedoors.com/index.php?showtopic=25 (in possession of author); Yahoo *Disc-O-Teen* Discussion Group, no. 266. Zacherley remembered it this way: "Jim Morrison looked at our weird set and mumbled, 'This is the damnedest TV show I've ever seen.'" Quoted in Corey Kilgannon, "Once a Ghoul, Always a Ghoul," *New York Times*, October 9, 2012.

51. Donna N., Yahoo *Disc-O-Teen* Discussion Group, no. 889.

52. Scrivani, *"Good Night, Whatever You Are!"* 148.

53. Yahoo *Disc-O-Teen* Discussion Group, no. 309.

54. Yahoo *Disc-O-Teen* Discussion Group, no. 100.

55. Scrivani, *"Good Night, Whatever You Are!"* 148.

56. Yahoo *Disc-O-Teen* Discussion Group, no. 766.

57. Yahoo *Disc-O-Teen* Discussion Group, no. 492, for allusion to smoking pot for the first time while listening to *Sgt. Pepper*.

58. Yahoo *Disc-O-Teen* Discussion Group, nos. 274 and 299.

59. Scrivani, *"Good Night, Whatever You Are!"* 164–165.

60. Scrivani, *"Good Night, Whatever You Are!"* 166.

61. Yahoo *Disc-O-Teen* Discussion Group, nos. 191 and 618.

62. Scrivani, *"Good Night, Whatever You Are!"* 167.

63. Scrivani, *"Good Night, Whatever You Are!"* 167.

64. Yahoo *Disc-O-Teen* Discussion Group, no. 499.

65. Scrivani, *"Good Night, Whatever You Are!"* 168.

66. Yahoo *Disc-O-Teen* Discussion Group, nos. 337 and 632.

67. Yahoo *Disc-O-Teen* Discussion Group, no. 558.

68. Scrivani, *"Good Night, Whatever You Are!"* 81.

69. Scrivani, *"Good Night, Whatever You Are!"* 120.

70. Linda Pace in Scrivani, *"Good Night, Whatever You Are!"* 81.

5. THE UPSTAGE CLUB AND THE ASBURY PARK SCENE

1. See Carrie Potter-Devening, *For Music's Sake: Asbury Park's Upstage Club and Green Mermaid Cafe—The Untold Stories* (Bloomington, IN: Author House, 2011), 65.
2. Steven Van Zandt quoted in Potter-Devening, *For Music's Sake*, 111.
3. Southside Johnny in Gary Wien, *Beyond The Palace* (Victoria, B.C.: Trafford, 2003), loc. 322–336, Kindle.
4. Potter biographical material from Potter-Devening, *For Music's Sake*, 6–22.
5. Potter-Devening, *For Music's Sake*, 22.
6. Skip McGarry in Wien, *Beyond The Palace*, loc. 336–349.
7. Margaret Potter quoted in Susan Etta Keller, "Jamming on the Jersey Shore: A Community of Rock Musicians in Asbury Park, Its Formations and Traditions," *New Jersey Folklife* 13 (1988): 39.
8. Margaret Potter quoted in Potter-Devening, *For Music's Sake*, 103.
9. Potter-Devening, *For Music's Sake*, 20.
10. Joe Petillo in Potter-Devening, *For Music's Sake*, 79.
11. Petillo in Potter-Devening, *For Music's Sake*, 79.
12. Albee Tellone in Potter-Devening, *For Music's Sake*, 83.
13. David Mieras quoted in Wien, *Beyond The Palace*, loc. 309–322.
14. "New Discotheque Operators Feel Young Adults Are Their Business," *Asbury Park Sunday Press*, March 10, 1968, 42; printed in Potter-Devening, *For Music's Sake*, 102.
15. Tellone in Potter-Devening, *For Music's Sake*, 83.
16. Wien, *Beyond The Palace*, loc. 218–230.
17. Robbin Thompson quoted in Potter-Devening, *For Music's Sake*, 132–133.
18. Robbin Thompson in Keller, "Jamming on the Jersey Shore," 45.
19. Petillo in Potter-Devening, *For Music's Sake*, 79.
20. Southside Johnny in Wien, *Beyond The Palace*, loc. 322–336.
21. Tellone in Potter-Devening, *For Music's Sake*, 89.
22. Tellone in Potter-Devening, *For Music's Sake*, 91.
23. Vini "Mad Dog" Lopez in Potter-Devening, *For Music's Sake*, 91.
24. Keller, "Jamming on the Jersey Shore," 40.
25. Wien, *Beyond The Palace*, loc. 243–256.
26. Billy Ryan quoted in Potter-Devening, *For Music's Sake*, 148.
27. Wien, *Beyond The Palace*, loc. 256–269.
28. Thompson quoted in Potter-Devening, *For Music's Sake*, 133.
29. Keller, "Jamming on the Jersey Shore," 41.
30. Keller, "Jamming on the Jersey Shore," 41, 43.
31. Keller, "Jamming on the Jersey Shore," 43.
32. Sonny Kenn in Keller, "Jamming on the Jersey Shore," 42.
33. Robert Santelli in Keller, "Jamming on the Jersey Shore," 42.
34. Carmen quoted in Potter-Devening, *For Music's Sake*, 110.
35. Keller, "Jamming on the Jersey Shore," 43.
36. Gerry Carboy quoted in Potter-Devening, *For Music's Sake*, 132.

37. Santelli in Keller, "Jamming on the Jersey Shore," 43.

38. Kevin Kavanaugh quoted in Potter-Devening, *For Music's Sake*, 152.

39. Carboy quoted in Potter-Devening, *For Music's Sake*, 123.

40. Potter in Keller, "Jamming on the Jersey Shore," 44.

41. Wien, *Beyond The Palace*, loc. 256–269.

42. Wien, *Beyond The Palace*, loc. 256–269.

43. Springsteen and Potter quoted in Peter Ames Carlin, *Bruce* (New York: Touchstone, 2012), 50–51.

44. Springsteen quoted in Carlin, *Bruce*, 51.

45. Springsteen quoted in Carlin, *Bruce*, 51.

46. Geoff Potter quoted in Carlin, *Bruce*, 51–52.

47. Bruce Springsteen, *Born to Run* (New York: Simon and Schuster, 2016), 106.

48. Sonny Kenn quoted in Carlin, *Bruce*, 52.

49. Jim Fainer quoted in Carlin, *Bruce*, 52.

50. Carlin, *Bruce*, 53.

51. Springsteen, *Born to Run*, 106.

52. Vini Lopez quoted in Carlin, *Bruce*, 53.

53. Margaret Potter quoted in Potter-Devening, *For Music's Sake*, 117.

54. Wien, *Beyond The Palace*, loc. 283–296.

55. Tony Amato quoted in Wien, *Beyond The Palace*, loc. 363–376.

56. Wien, *Beyond The Palace*, loc. 296–309.

57. Billy Ryan quoted in Potter-Devening, *For Music's Sake*, 147.

58. Wien, *Beyond The Palace*, loc. 296–309.

59. David Mieras quoted in Wien, *Beyond The Palace*, loc. 309–322.

60. Potter-Devening, *For Music's Sake*, 94–95.

61. Carlin, *Bruce*, 91.

62. Bruce Springsteen, liner notes to Southside Johnny's album *I Don't Want to Go Home*.

63. Springsteen, liner notes.

64. Kevin Kavanaugh quoting Springsteen in Potter-Devening, *For Music's Sake*, 147.

65. Carlin, *Bruce*, 87.

66. Daniel Wolff, *4th of July, Asbury Park: A History of the Promised Land* (New York: Bloomsbury, 2005), 34–35.

67. See Katrina Martin, "The Asbury Park July 1970 Riots," June 28, 2016, http://blogs.library.duke.edu/rubenstein/2016/06/28/asbury-park-july-1970-riots/.

68. For an eloquent and insightful account of the riots, their place in Asbury Park history, and their aftermath, see Wolff, *4th of July, Asbury Park*, especially 180–190.

69. See Daniel Weeks, "From Riot to Revolt: Asbury Park in July 1970," *New Jersey Studies: An Interdisciplinary Journal* 2, no. 2 (Summer 2016), https://njs.libraries.rutgers.edu/index.php/njs/article/view/49.

70. J. T. Bowen quoted in Keller, "Jamming on the Jersey Shore," 45.

71. Craig Hansen Werner, *A Change Is Gonna Come: Music, Race & the Soul of America* (Ann Arbor: University of Michigan Press, 2006), 219.

72. Springsteen quoted in Werner, *Change Is Gonna Come*, 220.

73. David Sancious quoted in Wolff, *4th of July, Asbury Park*, 177.

74. Sancious quoted in Wolff, *4th of July, Asbury Park*, 179–180.

75. Wolff, *4th of July, Asbury Park*, 192.

76. Al Subarsky and Albee Tellone in Potter-Devening, *For Music's Sake*, 206–207.

77. Carboy in Potter-Devening, *For Music's Sake*, 208.

78. Jim Fanier in Potter-Devening, *For Music's Sake*, 213.

79. Bobby Williams in Keller, "Jamming on the Jersey Shore," 45.

80. Petillo in Potter-Devening, *For Music's Sake*, 202.

81. Potter-Devening, *For Music's Sake*, 224.

82. Sonny Kenn in Keller, "Jamming on the Jersey Shore," 48.

6. "DRUMS ALONG THE HUDSON"

1. Melissa Pierson, *The Place You Love Is Gone: Progress Hits Home* (New York: W. W. Norton, 2006), 70.

2. Pierson, *Place You Love Is Gone*, 74.

3. John Holl, "Hoboken in the '70s: Stayin' Alive," *New York Times*, February 25, 2007, http://www.nytimes.com/2007/02/25/nyregion/nyregionspecial2/25njpix.html.

4. Michael Azerrad, *Our Band Could Be Your Life: Scenes from the American Indie Underground, 1981–1991* (Boston: Little, Brown, 2001), 3.

5. Steve Fallon quoted in Craig Marks, "The Hoboken Sound: An Oral History of Maxwell's," *Vulture*, July 22, 2013, https://www.vulture.com/2013/07/hoboken-sound-an-oral-history-of-maxwells.html.

6. Jim Testa, "Author Jesse Jarnouw on Baseball, Hoboken History, and the Rise of Indie Rock at Hoboken Museum Presentation," *Jersey Journal*, December 7, 2012, http://www.nj.com/hobokennow/index.ssf/2012/12/author_jesse_jarnow_on_basebal.html.

7. Jim Testa, "Alice Genese and Karyn Kuhl Remember Maxwell's in the Eighties, Say Good-bye on Saturday," *Jersey Journal*, June 27, 2013, http://www.nj.com/hobokennow/index.ssf/2013/06/alice_genese_and_karyn_kuhl_re.html.

8. Pierson, *Place You Love Is Gone*, 76.

9. Terrence Dopp and Elizabeth Dexheimer, "Maxwell's Goes Dark as Hoboken Bar Where Nirvana Played Ends Run," *Bloomberg*, July 29, 2013, https://www.bloomberg.com/news/articles/2013-07-30/maxwell-s-goes-dark-as-hoboken-bar-where-nirvana-played-ends-run.

10. Glenn Morrow quoted in Marks, "Hoboken Sound."

11. Jane Wygal quoted in Marks, "Hoboken Sound."

12. Richard Barone, "Maxwell's: When the Club Was the Star," *Spin*, July 29, 2013, http://www.spin.com/2013/07/maxwells-club-closing-hoboken-richard-barone-bongos/.

13. Glenn Morrow quoted in Tris McCall, "Farewell, Maxwell's: Ending a Chapter in Hoboken's History, Iconic Rock Club Set to Close This Week," *Inside Jersey*, July 28, 2013, http://www.nj.com/entertainment/index.ssf/2013/07/farewell_maxwells_ending_a_chapter_in_hobokens_history_iconic_rock_club_set_to_close_this_week.html.

14. Morrow quoted in Marks, "Hoboken Sound."

15. Andy Newman, "End for Bar That Altered Music Scene, and Hoboken," *New York Times*, June 6, 2013, http://www.nytimes.com/2013/06/07/nyregion/at-maxwells-a-proving-ground-for-indie-music-acts-awe-at-a-35-year-run.html.

16. Collection of Rob Norris.

17. Will Rigby quoted in Marks, "Hoboken Sound."

18. Barone, "Maxwell's."

19. Steve Fallon quoted in McCall, "Farewell, Maxwell's."

20. Ira Kaplan quoted in Marks, "Hoboken Sound."

21. Karyn Kuhl quoted in Melissa Colangelo, "Karyn Kuhl," *hmag*, May 12, 2014, http://hmag.com/736/.

22. Mac McCaughan quoted in Marks, "Hoboken Sound."

23. Jim DeRogatis, "R.I.P. Maxwell's: Requiem for a Rock Club," *WBEZ.org*, June 4, 2013, https://www.wbez.org/shows/jim-derogatis/rip-maxwells-requiem-for-a-rock-club/54596e49-42ac-468d-9e4b-f1f0be11fb90.

24. The Bongos, *Drums Along the Hudson*, (orig. PVC, 1982) Jem Recordings, MVD6181A, CD, 2014. Liner notes by Matt Pinfield.

25. "The Bongos," *Trouser Press*, http://www.trouserpress.com/entry.php?a=bongos.

26. Robert Palmer, "Rock: Richard Barone," *New York Times*, December 16, 1987, http://www.nytimes.com/1987/12/16/arts/rock-richard-barone.html.

27. Jim Beckerman, "Maxwell's Goes, and with It an Era of Music in Hoboken," Northjersey.com, July 8, 2013, accessed July 18, 2016, http://archive.northjersey.com/arts-and-entertainment/music/maxwell-s-goes-and-with-it-an-era-of-music-in-hoboken-1.640354?page=all.

28. Ira A. Robbins, ed., *Rolling Stone Review 1985* (New York: Scribner, 1985), 89. https://books.google.com/books?id=3gowAQAAIAAJ&q=%22the+cucumbers%22+%22rolling+stone%22&dq=%22the+cucumbers%22+%22rolling+stone%22&hl=en&sa=X&ei=Qny_UtfEKIOvsQTpp4GgDQ&ved=0CEcQ6AEwBQ.

29. Robert Christgau, *Consumer Guide Reviews*, http://robertchristgau.com/get_artist.php?name=cucumbers.

30. Jon Pareles, "Pop: The Cucumbers, Group from Hoboken," *New York Times*, December 30, 1987, http://www.nytimes.com/1987/12/30/arts/pop-the-cucumbers-group-from-hoboken.html.

31. Bill Million quoted in Nate Rogers, "An Indirectly Direct History of The Feelies," *Flood Magazine*, July 5, 2016, http://floodmagazine.com/37580/tomorrow-today-an-indirectly-direct-history-of-the-feelies/.

32. Glenn Mercer quoted in Rogers, "Indirectly Direct History."

33. Glenn Mercer quoted in Brad Cohen, "The World Is Still Catching Up to the Genius Indie Rock The Feelies Ignited," *Observer*, July 18, 2016, http://observer.com/2016/07/the-world-is-still-catching-up-to-the-genius-indie-rock-the-feelies-ignited/.

34. Mercer quoted in Cohen, "World Is Still Catching Up."

35. Jim Testa, "Maxwell's: Jim Testa Says Good-Bye," *Jersey Beat* (ca. August 2013), http://www.jerseybeat.com/maxwells-bye.html.

36. Mary Marcus in "Bar/None's First Intern (1986)," Bar None 30th Anniversary blog, April 10, 2016, https://barnoneturns30.blogspot.com/2016/04/barnones-first-intern-1986_10.html.

37. Kate Jacobs, Bar None 30th Anniversary blog, April 8, 2016, https://barnoneturns30.blogspot.com/2016/04/kate-jacobs-calm-comes-after-1993-kate.html.

38. Glenn Morrow in "Bar/None's First Intern (1986)."

39. For a fond remembrance, see http://hiptran.typepad.com/blog/2009/02/pier-platters.html.

40. Jim DeRogatis, "Memories of Playing Maxwell's: 'The Bar in "Cheers" for Music Geeks,'" *Jersey Journal*, July 13, 2013, accessed October 16, 2016, http://www.nj.com/hudson/index.ssf/2013/07/memories_of_playing_maxwells_the_bar_in_cheers_for_music_geeks.html.

41. Fallon quoted in Marks, "Hoboken Sound."

42. Todd Abramson quoted in Marks, "Hoboken Sound."

43. Joel Rose, "Maxwell's, the Beloved New Jersey Venue, Closes," *NPR*, July 30, 2013, http://www.npr.org/templates/transcript/transcript.php?storyId=206669495.

44. Chris Rotolo, "Interview: Richard Barone (The Bongos) Reflects on Maxwell's and the Birth of a Hoboken Music Scene," *Speak into My Goodeye*, June 10, 2013, http://speakimge.com/interview-richard-barone-the-bongos-reflects-on-maxwells-and-the-birth-of-a-hoboken-music-scene/.

45. Bob Mould, *See a Little Light: The Trail of Rage and Melody* (New York: Little, Brown, 2011), 94.

46. Richard Barone, *Frontman: Surviving the Rock Star Myth* (New York: Backbeat Books, 2007), 59.

47. Fallon quoted in Marks, "Hoboken Sound."

48. Barone quoted in Marks, "Hoboken Sound."

49. Testa, "Alice Genese and Karyn Kuhl."

50. Testa, "Alice Genese and Karyn Kuhl."

51. Alice Genese quoted in Jesse Sposato, "An Ode to Maxwell's," *Rumpus*, July 30, 2014, http://therumpus.net/2014/07/an-ode-to-maxwells/ (accessed October 16, 2016).

52. Janet Wygal quoted in Sposato, "Ode to Maxwell's."

53. Pierson, *Place You Love Is Gone*, 76.

54. Fallon quoted in McCall, "Farewell, Maxwell's."

55. Todd Abramson quoted in Rose, "Maxwell's."

56. Steve Fallon quoted in Sposato, "Ode to Maxwell's."

57. DeRogatis, "R.I.P. Maxwell's."

58. Gerard Cosloy, "The Place That Ran Contrary To (Almost) Every Negative Rock Club Stereotype: A Fond Farewell To Maxwell's," *Can't Stop The Bleeding*, June 4, 2013, http://www.cantstopthebleeding.com/the-place-that-ran-contrary-to-almost-every-negative-rock-club-stereotype-a-fond-farewell-to-maxells.

59. Ronnie Barrett of the Muffs quoted in Sposato, "Ode to Maxwell's."

60. Testa, "Maxwell's."

61. Kapland quoted in Dopp and Dexheimer, "Maxwell's Goes Dark."

62. Paul Major and Peter Holsapple quoted in Sposato, "Ode to Maxwell's."

63. Peter Prescott quoted in Sposato, "Ode to Maxwell's."

64. Cosloy, "Place That Ran Contrary."

65. Testa, "Maxwell's."

66. Jim DeRogatis, "Memories of Playing Maxwell's."

67. Pierson, *Place You Love Is Gone*, 77.

68. Pierson, *Place You Love Is Gone*, 103

69. Christgau, *Consumer Guide Reviews*.

70. Jon Fried and Deena Shoshkes, "My Town," The Cucumbers (LP), Profile Records (New York, NY) 1987. Permission to quote "My Town" by the Cucumbers. © & ® Jon Fried (ASCAP) & Deena Shoshkes (ASCAP), 1987.

71. DeRogatis, "Memories of Playing Maxwell's."

72. Barone, "Maxwell's."

73. Karyn Kuhl quoted in Testa, "Alice Genese and Karyn Kuhl."

74. Newman, "End for Bar."

75. Pierson, *Place You Love Is Gone*, 107.

CONCLUSION

1. For an insightful academic account, see Andrew Berish, "From the 'Make-Believe Ballroom' to the Meadowbrook Inn: Charlie Barnet and the Promise of the Road," in *Lonesome Roads and Streets of Dreams: Place, Mobility, and Race in Jazz of the 1930s and '40s* (Chicago: University of Chicago Press, 2012), 73–118. See also Philip M. Read, *Memories from the Meadowbrook* (Gloucestershire: Fonthill Media, 2014); "The Meadowbrook Project," http://www.meadowbrookproject.com/about%20the%20meadowbrook.htm; "A Who's Who of Meadowbrook Performers," http://www.cedargrove.k12.nj.us/north /meadowbrook/index.htm; a student website created for Cedar Grove Centennial (2008), http://cgcentennial.typepad.com/cedar_grove_centennial/meadowbrook -whos-who.html; and Greg Hatala, "Glimpse of History: Teens Are All Ears in Cedar Grove," *Star-Ledger*, July 20, 2015, https://www.nj.com/essex/index.ssf/2015/07/glimpse _of_history_teens_are_all_ears_in_cedar_gro.html. See the discussion thread on H-New-Jersey, "A Few Folks Chime In on the Meadowbrook," January 29, 2011, http://h -net.msu.edu/cgi-bin/logbrowse.pl?trx=vx&list=h-new-jersey&month=1101&week =e&msg=GYrvj%2B1zeLO5%2B053LDR8uA&user=&pw=. For the television series, see the entry "Music from the Meadowbrook," in Wesley Hyatt, *Short-Lived Television Series, 1948–1978: Thirty Years of More Than 1,000 Flops* (Jefferson, NC: McFarland, 2003), 46.

2. Alec Wilkinson, "Live from New Jersey: D.I.Y. Dept," *New Yorker*, September 26, 2011, https://www.newyorker.com/magazine/2011/09/26/live-from-new-jersey. Tammy La Gorce, "Music Is in the House," *New Jersey Monthly*, March 13, 2012, https://njmonthly .com/articles/jersey-living/music-is-in-the-house/. See "Living Room Concerts: Welcome to Live at Drew's," *Fuse TV*, March 2, 2012, https://www.youtube.com/watch?v =ShLPLLkLBHc. For other house-concert series, see "Notes from Home House Concert

Series in Montclair," https://notesfromhomenj.com/ and Cabin Concerts out of Hawthorne at http://cabinconcerts.com/.

3. Christine A. Lutz, "Cabin in the Pines: Albert Music Hall and Constructions of a Pine Barrens Musical Tradition," *New Jersey Studies* 2, no. 2 (2016), http://dx.doi.org/10.14713 /njs.v2i2.47. See also Michael C. Gabriele, *New Jersey Folk Revival Music: History & Tradition* (Charleston, SC: History Press, 2016), 109–117. And "The Story of Albert Music Hall," https://www.alberthall.org/history. For more recent accounts of the contemporary "Saturday night scene" at Albert Music Hall, see Fred Goodman, "Lost in the Pines," *New Jersey Monthly*, September 13, 2011, https://njmonthly.com/articles/jersey-living/lost-in -the-pines/; and Margo Nash, "'Piney' Tunes: It's the Music of Old New Jersey," *New York Times*, March 10, 2002, https://www.nytimes.com/2002/03/10/nyregion/piney -tunes-it-s-the-music-of-old-jersey.html.

4. See http://www.njfolkfest.org/.

5. For a fascinating account of a man who books cover bands of the Jersey Shore, see A. D. Amorosi, "Cultivating the Cover Band Sound at the Jersey Shore," *Philadelphia Inquirer*, July 10, 2015, http://www.philly.com/philly/living/travel/shoreguide/20150710 _Cultivating_the_cover_band_sound_at_the_Jersey_Shore.html.

6. Barbara J. Kukla, *Swing City: Newark Nightlife, 1925–50* (New Brunswick, NJ: Rutgers University Press, 2002); Kukla, *America's Music: Jazz in Newark* (West Orange, NJ: Swing City Press, 2014); and Kukla, *The Encyclopedia of Newark Jazz: A Century of Great Music* (West Orange, NJ: Swing City Press, 2017). See also Tammy La Gorce, "How Newark Became One of the Greatest Jazz Cities in the World," *The Guardian*, November 11, 2016, https://www.theguardian.com/music/2016/nov/11/newark-new-jersey-jazz-institute -njpac-clements-place.

7. Amy Yates Wuelfing and Steven DiLodovico, "No Slam Dancing, No Stage Diving, No Spikes: An Oral History of the Legendary City Gardens" (Morrisville, PA: DiWulf Publishing, 2014). "Riot on the Dance Floor: The Story of Randy Now and City Gardens," directed by Steve Tozzi (Playfort Productions, 2014).

8. See http://www2.scc.rutgers.edu/ead/snjc/nbmsaf.html; and https://nbmusic scenearchive.tumblr.com/. See Christine A. Lutz, "Listening to the Local Beat: New Archive Documents New Brunswick Music Scene During Recent Decades," *Mid-Atlantic Archivist* 45, no. 3 (Summer 2016), https://marac.memberclicks.net/assets/maa /maracsummer16.pdf; and Maddie Orton, "New Brunswick Music Scene Takes Its Place in History," *NJTV News*, February 12, 2016, https://www.njtvonline.org/news/video /new-brunswick-music-scene-takes-its-place-in-history/. Ronen Kaufman, *New Brunswick, New Jersey, Goodbye: Bands, Dirty Basements, and the Search for Self* (Van Nuys, CA: Hopeless Records, 2007) offers a vivid first-person account. See also Bob Makin, "New Brunswick Rock Bands, Driven Underground, Thrive in Basement Scene," *NJArts.net*, April 20, 2017, https://www.njarts.net/pop-rock/new-brunswick-rock-bands-driven -underground-thrive-basement-scene/; and Sarah Beth Kaye, "New Brunswick Basements Ranked #4 Place to See Indie Bands in NJ," *New Brunswick Today*, September 3, 2014, http://newbrunswicktoday.com/article/new-brunswick-basements-ranked-4 -place-see-indie-bands-nj.

9. See http://vlhfilms.com/blog/new-brunswick-music-scene-documentary/; and Andrew Sacher, "New Brunswick Music Scene Subject of New Documentary," *Brooklyn Vegan*, April 24, 2017, http://www.brooklynvegan.com/new-brunswick-music-scene-subject-of-new-documentary-watch-a-new-trailer/.

10. Bob Cannon, "Montclair's Flemtones Celebrate 30 Years at Tierney's," *Montclair Times*, February 23, 1986, https://www.northjersey.com/story/news/essex/montclair/2016/02/23/montclairs-flemtones-celebrate-30-years-at-tierneys/94509020/.

11. See http://www.outpostintheburbs.org/.

12. "A Seat in the House: Outpost in the Burbs," *Wired Jersey* (2015), http://wiredjersey.com/a-seat-in-the-house-outpost-in-the-burbs/.

13. See https://www.montclairjazzfestival.org/; and https://jazzhousekids.org/. For a brief history of previous jazz festivals in Montclair, see Catherine Baxter, "Jazz Festivals of Montclair," *Montclair Dispatch*, June 11, 2015, https://montclairdispatch.com/jazz-festivals-of-montclair/.

14. Catherine Baxter, "DLV Lounge: Montclair's Hidden Gem," *Montclair Dispatch*, October 30, 2014, https://montclairdispatch.com/dlv-lounge/; and https://montclaircenter.com/dining/nightlife/dlv-lounge/.

15. See http://montclairmakesmusic.org/.

16. See http://www.makemusicday.org/.

17. Colin Moynihan, "For $1, a Collective Mixing Art and Radical Politics Turns Itself into Its Own Landlord," *New York Times*, July 4, 2006, https://www.nytimes.com/2006/07/04/nyregion/04abc.html. For more on ABC No Rio, see http://www.abcnorio.org/about/about.html; Alan W. Moore, "ABC No Rio as an Anarchist Space," in Tom Goyens, ed., *Radical Gotham: Anarchism in New York City from Schwab's Saloon to Occupy Wall Street* (Champaign: University of Illinois Press, 2017); Elie, "Demolition of ABC No Rio's Former HQ Commences on Rivington Street," *Bowery Boogie*, March 8, 2017, https://www.boweryboogie.com/2017/03/demolition-abc-no-rios-former-hq-commences-rivington-street/; James Timarco, "ABC No Rio," *Brooklyn Rail*, February 6, 2008, https://brooklynrail.org/2008/02/local/abc-no-rio; and Colin Moynihan, "ABC No Rio Gears Up for a Razing and a Brand-New Home," *New York Times*, May 16, 2016, https://www.nytimes.com/2016/05/17/arts/design/abc-no-rio-building-to-be-razed.html.

18. For local coverage, see Vicki Hyman, "Who Is Carl Lentz, the N.J. Pastor behind Justin Bieber, Kyrie Irving Controversies?" *NJ.Com*, July 26, 2017, https://www.nj.com/entertainment/celebrities/index.ssf/2017/07/who_is_carl_lentz_the_nj_pastor_behind_justin_bieb.html; Michael Sol Warren, "Meet Carl Lentz, N.J.'s Celeb Pastor Changing the Way We Think about Faith," *NJ.Com*, December 17, 2017, https://www.nj.com/entertainment/index.ssf/2017/12/bieber_irving_and_montclair_meet_pastor_carl_lentz.html; and Joshua Jongsma, "Montclair a Popular Destination for Justin Bieber," *NorthJersey.com*, June 30, 2017, https://www.northjersey.com/story/news/essex/montclair/2017/06/30/montclair-popular-destination-justin-bieber/442972001/.

19. Linda Moss, "Montclair Arts Groups Discuss Forming Alliance," *Montclair Local*, May 18, 2017, http://www.montclairlocal.news/wp/index.php/2017/05/18/montclair-arts-groups-discuss-forming-alliance/.

20. "HANDS Introduces the New Hat City, Get Ready!" July 28, 2017, https://handsinc
.org/hands-introduces-the-new-hat-city-get-ready/. See https://www.hatcitynj.com/;
David M. Halbfinger, "Cajun-Spiced Food, in a Nonprofit Setting," *New York Times*, January 14, 2011, https://www.nytimes.com/2011/01/16/nyregion/16dinenj.html; Patricia
Rogers, "The Next Chapter of Hat City Kitchen," Jersey Indie (n.d. ca. 2017), http://www
.jerseyindie.com/the-next-chapter-of-hat-city-kitchen/; and Donny Levit, "Revamped
Hat City in Orange Will Feature New Vibe, Menu and Music," *Village Green*, October 18,
2017, https://villagegreennj.com/arts/revamped-hat-city-orange-will-feature-new-vibe
-menu-music/.
21. Kevin Kiley, "Franklin Tavern Jam Celebrates One Year Anniversary," July 5, 2006,
https://groups.google.com/forum/#!topic/bit.listserv.blues-l/umCLCurCQcc; and
Nik Rael, "Real Blues at the Franklin Tavern," *Jersey Tomato Press*, July 23, 2009, http://
thejerseytomatopress.com/stories/Real-Blues-at-the-Franklin-Tavern,1322.
22. Bob Cannon, "A Place Where the Kids Are Alright," *Montclair Times*, August 6, 2015,
http://tulavera.com/images/20150806montclairtimes.pdf.
23. Nick quoted in "Don't Hang on the Pipes: 30 Years of Legacy at the Meatlocker,"
May 16, 2017, *Head Walk*, http://www.theheadwalk.com/2017/05/16/dont-hang-pipes
-30-years-legacy-meatlocker/.
24. Peter August, personal communication to author, June 16, 2017.
25. Peter August, personal communication to author.
26. Steve from Tru quoted in "Don't Hang on the Pipes."
27. Nicole quoted in "Don't Hang on the Pipes."
28. Peter August, personal communication to author.
29. Peter August, personal communication to author.

INDEX

Italic page numbers indicate illustrations.

ABOUT THE AUTHOR

DEWAR MACLEOD is a professor of history at William Paterson University and author of *Kids of the Black Hole: Punk Rock in Postsuburban California*. He sings and plays guitar for Thee Volatiles, the greatest punk rock band in Montclair, New Jersey.